Praise for
Made for Brave

I couldn't put this book down! It was truly an honor to read Alyssa's story of great loss and grief and how her God so lovingly walked alongside her and rescued her from the darkness. I am a better person for reading this book, and I know you will be too. Peace, joy, triumph, and hope are found on these pages, and I'm forever grateful for these words.

—Alyssa Bethke, author of *Love That Lasts*

Made for Brave is an incredible story of beauty from ashes. It is a reminder that God never forsakes us, no matter what storms and darkness we encounter, and that in His goodness, He makes all things beautiful—whether we get to witness it in this momentary life or not. It is a story of hope that encourages every person to cling to God and turn to His light when all other lights have gone out."

—Kevin Kim, executive director at *Crazy Love*

People everywhere *need* to hear Alyssa's story. If you feel alone or lost in your darkest moments, or are simply searching for an extra bit of hope, read this beautifully written story about love, loss, and new beginnings."

—Carla Marie, host of the *Carla Marie and Anthony Morning Show*

Alyssa's journey is truly one of bravery, strength, and resilience. *Made For Brave* will leave all women with a renewed faith in God and a reminder that there is a much bigger picture and purpose for each and every one of our lives.

—Sarah Ordo, author of *Innerbloom*

Reading Alyssa's story, I found myself with a broken heart that was simultaneously filled with *hope*. After reading *Made for Brave*, I am more inspired than ever to let go and let God, to see the silver linings in the darkness, and to appreciate the life I'm living *now* and the people in it.

—Tatum Garino, editor in chief, *This Is . . . Magazine*

Incredible! *Made for Brave* is an absolute must-read, and within seconds you will be hooked! This is truly one of the most inspiring stories you'll ever have the privilege of reading.

—Johnathon Stone, author of *Finding Good*

Made for Brave is a real and raw redemption story and a shining example of the beautiful truth that God desires to work *all* things together for the good of those who love Him. As a fellow widow, I could not put it down! It is just so encouraging to read Alyssa's testimony and see how God worked all the pieces together to create a beautiful story. Alyssa is proof that even our tragedies can be turned into triumphs when we relinquish our own plans and control and choose to live bravely by partnering with God and allowing Him to move.

—Ashley Cochrane, founder of Crowned for Ashes

Inspiring and life changing. Alyssa deals with the deepest recesses of grief and despair through the eyes of hope and God's transformative love. A must-read for anyone who has experienced grief and loss or for anyone who knows someone who has gone through the loss of a loved one.

—Jessica Lincoln, author of *Freak, Geek, Goddess*

The story you'll read here is not just about Alyssa's extraordinary experience of faith and trust or Nick's indelible confidence in Christ, but it's also about the Savior who stared death in the face on the cross so that we might all share in the hope of a resurrected life.

—Reverend Eric Spangler

I could not stop reading it once I started! In raw and honest detail, Alyssa masterfully shares her journey to make sense of faith's hardest issues. This thoroughly inspiring book avoids platitudes and easy answers and replaces them with hope and true faith.

—Dan Hamer, senior associate pastor at
Overlake Christian Church

In a world where there are no answers to the pain, Alyssa Galios shares with riveting vulnerability how she walked through the valley of the shadow of death to the other side. Her discovery of a love relationship with the surprising God who loved her all along is one you don't want to miss. This book will break your heart, and refresh your soul.

—Karen Johnson, senior associate in leadership development
at Centered.org

More than a memoir, *Made for Brave* is an intimate look at life, love, heartbreak, and hope. Alyssa Galios bravely shares her courageous journey through loss with grace, truth, and beauty. Honest and exquisitely written, this book will be a tremendous inspiration and a source of strength for anyone affected by life's greatest challenges.

—June Leahy, executive director at the Austen Everett
Foundation

I don't think Alyssa sets out to teach the reader anything. Instead, she does something better. She tells her story as honestly as she can and reminds us that life is happening for us not tomorrow, not later, but *right now*. Through tragedy and loss, and finding love and connection again through the blessings of our Creator, Alyssa shows us what it really means to live with heaven in your heart.

—Kat Kim, founder of School of Divine Confidence

Alyssa is a living, breathing example of a transparent life, and this book is the epitome of that. *Made for Brave* is an easy read and will readily inspire anyone who reads it with the message that God doesn't waste even a single step in one's life.

—Laura Inglis, LICSW, founder of Serenity Hope Counseling

The path you'll walk with Alyssa is one of the most faith-jerking, heart-crushing, yet God-redeeming journeys of raw, real life. The lessons I've taken from this book remind me that there truly is a divine plan created for each of us and it's most likely different than the ones we've imagined.

—Larry Snyder, author of *Which One Am I*

Alyssa Galios has an irresistible zest for life and a deep, honest belief that everyone has the capacity to find that happiness and the future they've always dreamed of. Her belief isn't contrived or fake. It draws you in. This is the story of how that energy and positivity was born. Her first book is raw and honest; you will laugh and most definitely cry. Her relationship with and understanding of God is inclusive and profound, and she offers it without hesitation and with a grace rarely seen. Read this book and you will walk away with a deep desire to seek the very best in your own life.

—Jeni Craswell, vice president of advancement at Hopelink

The strength it took to endure such a heartbreaking story is unimaginable. To see someone go through it and remain a force of hope and positivity is inspiring. Excited to see how many people Alyssa can reach and the effect this story will have."

—Sean Mackin, lead violinist, *Yellowcard*

MADE
FOR
Brave

A JOURNEY THROUGH
DEVASTATING LOSS
TO INFINITE HOPE

MADE
FOR
Brave

A JOURNEY THROUGH
**DEVASTATING LOSS
TO INFINITE HOPE**

A TRUE STORY BY
ALYSSA GALIOS

ROMANS 8:28
BOOKS

Published by Romans 8:28 Publishing, and imprint of Redemption Press, PO Box 427, Enumclaw, WA 98022.

Toll-Free (844) 2REDEEM (273-3336)

Redemption Press is honored to present this title in partnership with the author. The views expressed or implied in this work are those of the author. Redemption Press provides our imprint seal representing design excellence, creative content, and high quality production.

Unless otherwise noted, all Scripture quotations are taken from the *Christian Standard Bible*®, copyright © 2017 by Holman Bible Publishers. Used by permission. Christian Standard Bible® and CSB® are federally registered trademarks of Holman Bible Publishers.

Front cover "Brave" calligraphy by Claire Braby.

ISBN 13: 978-1-7329625-3-8 (Hardback)
          978-1-7329625-5-2 (ePub)
          978-1-7329625-4-5 (Mobi)

Library of Congress Catalog Card Number: 2019910492

Dedication

For Nick
You make me want to be braver still.
Proverbs 3:5–6

Content

Introduction

WHAT MAKES YOU THINK *anyone wants to hear your story?*

That's what the voices inside my head screamed at me while I prepared to write this book. But I've slowly come to realize something as I've poured my heart out in blog posts and across social media platforms for almost a decade: I'm not the only one.

I'm not the only one with negative thoughts swirling in my head.

I'm not the only one deathly afraid of dreaming big or loving again.

And I'm *definitely* not the only one who has doubted God's existence or His love.

I believe I've been called to share this story, to share my journey, because there is at least one person out there who needs to hear it. Now I have no idea how *you* ended up here, my friend, but I do not think you're here by accident. I believe you are meant to be holding this particular book in your hands at this specific point in your life.

That being said, you should know before we go any further that I'm not the kind of person who will tell you "Everything happens for a reason."

Nope. Not that.

Definitely not that.

I do believe it's entirely possible, though, to partner with the Creator of the universe to *create* meaning out of anything that happens. I'll even go as far as to say we can create *good* out of anything that happens. Yes, even the bad things.

Don't worry, whatever you believe or don't believe, you are welcome here. I used to be full of skepticism over this whole creating good out of bad thing, and I definitely didn't think this way when my own worst nightmare came true. So much happened in such a short period of time that proved me wrong though. So get comfy and buckle up because I'm going to share it with you now as well as I can remember as if we are a pair of old friends talking over coffee. I should probably also warn you that some of this might require a box of tissues, but I promise if you stick with me through the hard stuff, you'll read right on through to the miracles.

Wherever you happen to find yourself in your own journey, I believe this story will help you realize what's possible and finally see once and for all that you were always *made for brave* too.

This is a true story. This is my life. Welcome to it.

xo,

Alyssa

Chapter ONE

I Used to Think Doctors Knew Everything

September 20, 2011

I'VE HEARD PEOPLE SAY your world can turn upside down in an instant, but I didn't realize the devastating truth of those words until the day it happened to me.

The phone rang at my desk on a regular old Tuesday afternoon as I sat trying to work out the terms of a new contract. I glanced through the glass panel of my office door and made eye contact with the receptionist at the front desk. It was unusual for her to send calls straight through to me when she knew I was working a deal. *Odd*, I thought as she frantically motioned for me to pick up, a look of concern etched across her face. Wondering who in the world it might be, I answered, "This is Alyssa."

"Love, I need you to come get me. Something's wrong."

My heart skipped at the panicked sound of my husband's voice.

"Your stomach?" It was my best guess.

"Yes! *Please hurry!*"

I grabbed my purse from under my desk and threw open the office door, not even stopping to save the contract or grab my jacket. I was never one to leave in the middle of the workday, but the desperation in my husband's voice sent chills straight down my spine.

"I need to go. Nick needs help!" I called over my shoulder as I sprinted past my boss and through the lobby.

I practically fell down three flights of stairs, jumped into my car, and peeled out of the parking garage, cursing under my breath. Dialing Nick's number, I demanded he stay on the phone with me as I made my way toward the dealership where he worked as a service advisor in Bellevue, just east of Seattle.

We'd gone to the doctor just three days before, only the second doctor's visit Nick had been to in the four years since we'd met. He rarely even caught a common cold. After some questions and customary tests, the physician had assured us Nick was, without a doubt, 100 percent fine. My tall, dark, and handsome twenty-four-year-old hubby was "healthy as a horse."

"The pain could be from a stomach virus," the doctor said. "To be honest, it could even just be bad food or something. You wouldn't believe how many patients come through with stomach problems and later on find it's just . . . gas."

Nick and I looked at each other and couldn't help but burst out laughing, relieved to hear his discomfort might just be due to our diet, which was admittedly high in Mexican takeout.

But now on the phone with me, Nick's voice sounded strained past the point of bad salsa. "I've never felt anything like this before. Something is wrong." He said the dull ache from days before had never fully gone away and had instead turned into severe and constant agony. When he described the sharp discomfort and location to his doctor over the phone, the doctor told Nick to come to his office immediately.

I punched the gas, willing our Scion TC to go as fast as possible. *Please, God, don't let me get pulled over. Not now.*

When I pulled up to Nick's work ten minutes later, I spotted him right away, limping out a back door, struggling to walk. I jumped out of the car and sprinted over to him, wishing I wasn't in heels. Bracing myself, I let him use my five-foot-three-inch body as a crutch.

After easing him into the passenger seat with quite a bit of effort, I threw the car into drive. I'd never seen him like this. Nick was the strong one. He was the happy, smiling, optimistic one. And he was always, without a doubt . . . the *healthy* one.

Ours had been a whirlwind romance, like one of those Hallmark movies complete with an early onset of seemingly insurmountable challenges. We met when we were practically babies. I was nineteen; Nick was twenty. Struggles aside, I thought I'd hit the jackpot when he proposed six months after we met.

Our wedding was small, but in all the ways that truly mattered, it was perfect. I was thrilled to be marrying the man of my dreams. Handsome as they come, Nick had an amazing smile and the magical ability to make everyone around him feel important, especially me. He was unfailingly kind and, as was necessary for my parents' approval, he loved God with his whole heart.

But not long after our incredible honeymoon, the novelty of our relationship faded right along with our tans. What had started out as a whirlwind romance and fantastical soulmate matchup quickly turned into something else entirely. Eventually we found ourselves forcing down bites of the frozen top of our wedding cake, and before we knew it, it had been not just one but three years since we'd said, "I do."

We worked insane hours in those first several years of marriage. Nick started out moving cars around the lot at a local showroom; I began at the front desk of a personal training facility. Both of us were self-motivated and hard workers, and as we started climbing up our respective corporate ladders, our working hours climbed too.

The more I found myself focusing on my career goals, the more my appreciation for the small joys of life seemed to disappear. And after a couple of years, so did much of my appreciation for Nick.

To add to the mix, social media, the mother of all discontentment, arrived on the scene. I began comparing my life to what I saw while scrolling Pinterest boards and Facebook news feeds. I did it subconsciously, but I did it *a lot*, comparing *everything*.

Nothing was off limits in my mind: my ring, our jobs, our relationship, or our incredibly expensive but undeniably rundown city-living condo. Both Nick and I felt a little behind when we compared our achievements to those of our friends and the highlight reels online just made it worse. Social media, of course, is not all bad, but the way I used it was. We all know comparison can steal our joy, but it did worse to me—it made me miserable.

My own personal discontentment crept up on me so slowly I barely even noticed it was happening. Eventually it got so bad that I convinced Nick we should bundle together all of our savings and buy a house. We settled on one much too large for us and a whole commute away. I should have learned an expensive lesson when not even the big house made me happy. While my friends saw me as mostly optimistic, behind closed doors I had some serious issues to work on. Mastering contentment was *definitely* one of them.

About a month before I found myself speeding down the freeway toward my sick husband, our third wedding anniversary, August 16, 2011, had been right on the horizon. I'd perused Pinterest for weeks whenever I had free time, nailing the perfect gift for Nick with time to spare. Of course, I also came across all kinds of things that would have been perfect for *me*.

Much to my internet-loving dismay, when the morning of our anniversary finally came, all I got was a quick peck on the cheek. No jewelry. No breakfast in bed. No card next to my pillow. Not even a quick, "Happy Anniversary." Just like every other early morning, we'd rolled out of bed and slumped into our cars clutching our coffees for dear life, only to sit in an hour of bumper-to-bumper traffic. Our lives consisted of long commutes and even longer days working toward promotions and raises, all to pay for a house we were hardly ever at.

Though that morning had been rushed, I'd held on to hope for what could happen after work. I tried not to picture anything too spectacular. But, at the very least, I expected a nice card and reservations at a decent place.

As soon as I got home, after leaving the office on time for once, I set Nick's card and his carefully wrapped present on the counter. I'd discovered the traditional gift for a third-year anniversary was leather, so I'd ordered him a trendy leather wallet weeks in advance and tucked a sappy love note inside.

Maybe tonight will be our turning point, I thought. I could feel we'd been growing apart, but I hadn't stopped to identify the reasons why. In hindsight, I can see our insane work hours and my lack of appreciation for basically everything had pooped all over our relationship. We weren't making each other a priority. Our main concern, whether we wanted to admit it or not, was work. And our second? Also work. Whatever I might have thought my priorities were, the way I spent my time proved otherwise.

My phone buzzed with a text from Nick saying he'd be stopping by the store on his way home. *No big. He's probably picking up flowers! Or maybe champagne?* But when he got home a half an hour later, all I saw in his hand was a sagging plastic drugstore bag.

A few minutes later he handed me . . . a card. Below the generic preprinted sentiment was a bland two-sentence note he had scribbled in a hurry. No gift. No note about something in the mail or anything to look forward to. He'd just bought me a card on his way home . . . from the same place I got my birth control. *Oi.*

I did my best to keep my cool. I wanted to give him the benefit of the doubt. I mean, this was my *Nick.* He was usually so thoughtful! He certainly had to have *something* planned to celebrate the three years we'd been married.

"Um . . . thanks, babe," I said, attempting not to look too disappointed as I tucked the card back into its envelope and pushed my gift his way. I didn't want to believe he had forgotten the day I'd spent weeks looking forward to.

Nick's smile was huge as he unwrapped his gift. "This is perfect, love! Thank you!" He immediately pulled his old, tattered wallet out of his back pocket and started switching all of his cards over to the new one. He even got all choked up when he found my note.

"You're welcome, babe!" I paused a moment, but when he didn't say anything else, I asked, "So . . . should I go get ready? What should I wear?"

"For what?" At first he looked genuinely confused and then a bit guilty.

I was probably starting to look really annoyed. I couldn't believe this was happening. My husband hadn't made any plans for our anniversary.

"We have to go *somewhere* or do *something!*" I told Nick, now completely frustrated. "I'm going upstairs to change. You just . . . pick a place!"

I stamped up the stairs, gritting my teeth, determined to salvage what was left of our anniversary. Twenty minutes later I was in a dress, and I'd even gone as far as to run a straightener over my hair, mainly to give myself a few more minutes to calm down. I was pretty upset, but there was *no way* we were calling this a night.

We left the house, but, oh, how I wished we would have just stayed home. When Nick pulled into the parking lot of a dinky restaurant five miles from our house on the bottom floor of an empty office building located on the edge of a stormwater retention pond, I burst into a legit ugly cry.

You know the kind. Snot. Tears. Probably a little drool. All the built-up hurt came out at once after years of ignoring the tough conversations, setting high expectations only to be let down again and again, and comparing what other husbands did for their wives to what my husband did for me. It felt like everything was pointing to one fact: Nick no longer loved me.

"Do you even care about me at all?" My lip quivered as I wiped my eyes, trying to get it together.

When he attempted an apology, I scoffed, brushing it aside. *I can't believe this!*

I felt incredibly hurt, but I was also incredibly hungry, which was rapidly gaining in importance, so despite my smeared mascara, we went in. Nick was still in his suit from work, and I was wearing a dress. But, kid you not, everyone else seemed to have just come in from working on the farm.

We didn't tell the waitress *why* we were there, and she didn't ask, which was weird considering our attire. It should have been an easy conversation starter, but she probably sensed our tension from a mile away. I ordered a bacon cheeseburger with extra-greasy fries because the night was already blown, and I figured I might as well eat what I wanted (aka my feelings).

It's safe to say the mood that night was anything but romantic or celebratory. And it definitely wasn't the new start I'd been hoping for in our relationship.

As I lay awake all that night, I wondered, *Did I make a mistake in marrying Nick?* Maybe I had married a man who didn't love or cherish me after all. Maybe we *were* too young. Maybe we weren't cut out for this.

We'd been fighting a lot, arguing over the most trivial things—like laundry, and bills, and things that hadn't even happened yet and probably never would. Plus, the spark between us was so dim I couldn't even have called it a flicker if I wanted to.

Everything about being married had been one thousand times harder than I imagined it would be, and I couldn't picture fifty more anniversaries like this one.

"Was this really your plan, God? It kind of sucks," I whispered into the dark.

I didn't hear a response.

We pulled into the parking lot of the doctor's office with a loud screech. Once inside, I pulled Nick's health insurance card out of his new leather wallet and handed it to the lady at the front desk.

A nurse whisked Nick away as I was talking to the receptionist about how to fill out the form for an abdominal CT scan. Nick turned to say, "I'll be right back" and tried to smile my way, but it turned into more of a grimace as he doubled over in pain. He looked up just in time to mouth "I love you" before disappearing behind a set of automatic doors. Suddenly I was all alone. The paperwork filled out, all I could do was wait.

Some twenty minutes later, not knowing what else to do, I found myself staring at the carpet and trying to find a pattern in the multicolored fibers to keep my sanity. When the door opened and I saw Nick, I breathed a massive sigh of relief. My brain had already worked out a couple of scenarios that really weren't good.

"I don't need a wheelchair," Nick said to the nurse as he limped his way back to me, breathing hard. He could be so darn stubborn. It used to bother me, but eventually I would be grateful for that same stubbornness that would keep him fighting against impossible odds.

When doors flew open again a few moments later, a doctor rushed into the waiting room waving what I'm assuming were CAT scan results. "You need to get to the ER right now! Your appendix ruptured," he said urgently, looking directly at Nick. And then more quietly, he muttered, "I don't understand it."

"He should be dead." The doctor was staring at me now. "You need to take him to the ER. *Immediately*. We're right across the street and you taking him will be quicker than us calling an ambulance. Don't stop for anything. Just go!"

But for a few seconds, I didn't go. I didn't move. I just sat there.

I played soccer my whole life and my coaches always commended my ability to pivot and make quick decisions out on the field. At work, I was often praised for operating at top performance under pressure. But in the waiting room of a doctor's office as my husband's life seemingly hung in the balance, my reaction time was definitely delayed.

When I finally got my mind and body to cooperate, I gripped Nick's hand and started moving. We inched toward the door, him moving slowly because of the pain. Nurses gathered around the exit to watch the drama unfold, but I was barely aware of them. Nick was smiling and kept refusing the wheelchair they kept offering. I felt like I was in an episode of *The Twilight Zone*. I could almost hear the theme music playing as Nick and I moved in what felt like slow motion when I knew we should have been sprinting. My brain was going a million miles an hour despite the heavy, sinking feeling in the pit of my stomach.

Nick remained calm, cool, and collected the entire time. His face was a bit pale from the pain, but other than that, he looked like one of those perfectly chiseled statues you'd see in Italy. *How does he always manage to do that?* I wondered.

He tried to hold himself upright as we made our way back to the parking lot. He turned, smirking at me as I studied him hard. His dark-brown eyes crinkled a bit at the corners, his mouth turned upward in one of his infamous grins.

"I'm not dying, Alyssa. I don't know why the doctor was freaking out. It hurts, but it's not *that* bad. I'm going to be just fine."

Nick was pretty convincing. Always had been. I felt the tiniest bit relieved. If Nick thought he would be fine, then he would be. Life would go back to normal after this nightmare was over. Our recent normal hadn't exactly been a fairytale, but at least it was predictable. There was never a need to be brave. Even if it was a little boring, it was better than this mayhem.

When we were just ten feet from the car, Nick doubled over in pain again, erasing any doubts I held about the doctor's diagnosis.

Something was definitely wrong. This was *not* normal.

After pulling a "California stop" at every intersection I encountered, we arrived at Evergreen Hospital's Emergency Room just a few blocks away. Nick's doctor must have called ahead and told them we were coming because ER nurses were waiting just inside the door.

"Nicholas Magnotti?" a brunette with a clipboard asked. The second nurse, tall and blond, hurried over with yet another wheelchair.

"Yes, I'm Nick . . . but I don't need that," Nick said, refusing transportation yet again. "I prefer to walk." He flashed a defiant grin my way and winked.

My cheeks turned red as regret surged through me. His smile used to make me weak in the knees, but lately it barely made a dent in my hardened heart.

I tried to wink back, but I'd never really been great at winking. Plus, I was still trying not to cry. I'm not sure what was going on with my face in that moment, but I am certain it wasn't attractive. Nick was gazing at me with what seemed like complete adoration. *Has he looked at me like that at any point in the last month? What about the last two years of our marriage? Have I been missing something?*

Once Nick's vitals were checked, the concern in the nurses' eyes subsided, but only by a little.

"Let's get you into a room," the brunette said quickly.

"Finally! I was just starting to think you guys weren't taking me seriously!" Nick's smile rose right up to his eyes, and he let out a laugh.

I couldn't help but giggle in spite of my worry. He sure had a way of breaking the tension. *Man, I've forgotten how much I love him.*

The nurse led us through a swinging door, around a corner, and into a temporary "room" which consisted of floor-length curtains hung neatly around a hospital bed, a rolling cabinet of medical supplies, and some monitoring equipment.

A young male doctor showed up just as I was forcing my shaky fingers to tie the last bow on the back of Nick's hospital gown. He asked some questions mostly centered on Nick's gastrointestinal history. Of course, Nick made a few references to all the tacos we'd been eating, and I laughed harder than I meant to.

But the next words out of the ER doctor's mouth brought me back to reality and wiped the smile clean off my face.

"Nick, you should be sweating, screaming, vomiting, and passing out. Dying, to be honest. I've reviewed your scans and you have a burst appendix. But none of your symptoms support that theory. Your blood is normal. You seem relatively fine, but you're not." He studied my husband as if he were a tricky calculus problem he was determined to solve.

"So that means . . ." I asked, urging him to get to the point.

"I have no idea."

Well, at least he's honest.

The entire ER staff seemed just as baffled as the physician was who sent us there. Doctor after doctor stepped behind the enclosure to ask questions and to poke and prod. At one point, we had five medical professionals in our curtained space all at once, discussing Nick's case, offering suggestions, and attempting to make a plan. During one such medical powwow, another wave of pain washed over Nick's face, and I watched helplessly as the nurses did what they could to reposition him. I held his hand but mostly just felt in the way.

The hospital didn't have a clue what to do with us. Nick's scans showed a ruptured appendix but other than the exploded organ and the constant ebb and flow of intense abdominal pain, nothing seemed out of place. After almost five hours, it was obvious we weren't getting any closer to answers.

A nurse came by to deliver the news. "You guys will need to spend the night. We're moving you to an extended stay room on the fifth floor. It's the oncology floor, just to warn you."

"Oncology? That's cancer, right?" I asked.

"Right. But it's just the floor where we have space for you guys right now. Don't worry!"

On the way up the elevator, Nick had the nurse chatting about her job, life, and dreams for her children. He always knew how to make other people feel seen. As I followed behind them down the long hallway, I couldn't help but peek in the rooms we passed. The beds were filled with patients missing their hair and hooked up to machines and monitors by tubes and cords. I saw partners and family members who looked absolutely exhausted.

What a miserable place to be, I thought. I couldn't imagine what it might be like to spend days on end in a hospital. I frowned, shooting up a quick prayer for the patients and their families before we settled into a room at the end of the hall. Luckily, we'd be out of here soon. This floor gave me the creeps.

As hours turned into the next day, my adrenaline still hadn't started to fade. I didn't sleep a wink, and my heart raced, yet there I sat with nothing I could to do fix the situation. My whole life I had always disliked having nothing to do. Even during my soccer years, I didn't often ride the bench. Our hospital stay reminded me of those few games when I wasn't well enough to participate and had to sit on the sidelines. I absolutely hated it. I wanted to be in the game, to help my team, to contribute, but I was forced to watch instead.

This felt much the same. It was as if Nick and I had just experienced the craziest, most adrenaline-pumping "first half" and now we were benched. I was tense and ready to fight, but there was nothing to fight against.

I was already a little anxious because of the circumstances, but even a normal person could go crazy in a room that small with all the machines, the medical equipment, and the horrible antiseptic smell. So we did whatever we could to keep our heads. In the first twenty-four hours, I felt pretty dang productive aside from the problem at hand. If we weren't going to get anywhere with the doctors, I would at least get stuff done for work. Nick prayed; I responded to emails. I read; Nick made up silly songs. When I ran out of menial tasks, we played games with visiting friends and family. I also ate as much chocolate pudding as I could sneak from the kitchen without anyone really noticing.

After all that, there was still time. Lots of it. And Nick and I used it to talk. Hours upon hours of sitting together on Nick's hospital bed finally gave us the therapy we'd been needing for almost two years. For the first time in what felt like forever, we got it all out in the open. We laughed.

We cried. We talked about our marriage. About our jobs. About what mattered. We came clean about how we were feeling. Most importantly, we apologized and forgave each other for all the miscommunication over the years. As we talked, I was relieved to find Nick wanted a new beginning for us too.

We should have gotten real with each other and talked like that sooner. I had spent way too much time thinking about the lack of romance in our lives and then blaming Nick for not making the effort, instead of talking about it and telling him what I wanted. I assumed his actions, or lack thereof, meant he didn't love me. As it turned out, he had *no* idea I felt so bad—because I never told him.

By the end of the second night, we were emotionally drained but there was a new spark in the room, a glimmer of hope. Being stuck in the hospital, we decided, didn't have to be just a bad thing after all. This could be the start of something new. Our second chance. Even in the midst of all the uncertainty, for the first time in a long time, I felt excited about our relationship.

"I love you. I'm going to work on things. We *will* do better." Nick leaned down to kiss me on the forehead. We were snuggled up in his hospital bed, his pain pretty well managed at that point. I was feeling a little more like myself after brushing my teeth and changing into the pajamas my mom had brought over from our house the day before. "We'll always keep getting better together, love," he said. "I promise I won't ever stop trying. Forever and a day, right?"

"Forever and a day." I whispered back the sentiment we'd used so often early in our relationship when we had sworn over and over again that eternity wasn't long enough, so we would always add a day. Cuddling in closer, I rested my head on Nick's chest as he dozed off.

But every time I closed my eyes, questions raced and wouldn't stop. *What in the world is wrong with Nick? And what is wrong with me that it took me this long to remember how incredible he is?*

Alone with my thoughts, I couldn't help myself from questioning God over and over again. *How long will You keep this up?* I'd believed in Him wholeheartedly since I was a kid. I'd grown up in church. I'd even accepted Jesus as my Savior and gotten baptized at age nine. My parents were both believers: Dad since forever and Mom since she converted from being Catholic. But, over the last couple of years, everything had started to feel different. Anything to do with God, rubbed me raw. How could the God who "loved me" let things like *this* keep happening?

First, I'd gotten sick. Then, the thing with my parents. More recently, my own marriage had been falling apart. Now when it felt like our relationship was finally coming back together, something was definitely still wrong with my husband.

I whispered my prayers that night, tears streaming down my cheeks, believing God was listening but starting to wonder if He really cared. "God . . . heal Nick. You know what's wrong. Fix him. Please! I've been so focused on the wrong things. God, I'm begging You . . . I need another chance."

Chapter TWO

I Used to Be the Sick One

GROWING UP, I WAS one of those overachieving and annoying straight-A kids who loved school. I wrote my first "book" (a riveting ten-page number about a cat and a mouse) when I was in kindergarten and started my own business selling "potted plants" (uprooted dandelions in plastic cups) around the same time. Dad describes me back then as "inquisitive, rambunctious, but compassionate." Mom says I was "definitely a leader, fun-loving and adventurous, sweet but also strong-willed and stubborn."

Overall, my parents and most people who knew me would agree that I was a pretty friendly kid. But my freckles, poor eyesight, and crazy teeth that would require braces in the sixth grade, along with my love for schoolwork, kept me more in with the smarty-pants kids than the popular crowd. I didn't mind though. I didn't think I liked many of the things that a lot of the well-known girls seemed to enjoy anyway, like makeup, or dresses, or shopping. I loved sports and absolutely *lived* for adventures that put dirt under my fingernails.

Most of my favorite childhood memories are set in the great outdoors outside the home my parents built on almost five acres of wild forest about forty-five minutes north of Seattle. My brother, Jordan (two years younger); sister, Kinslee (four years younger); and I spent countless hours building forts in the woods, racing bikes with neighborhood kids, and making up elaborate games to which only we knew the rules. We didn't have cable television, just an old VHS player with a couple dozen movies, but I was never bored. Whenever I had free time, I always knew what to do with it—because there were always more woods to explore or books to read.

During the summer, if I wasn't playing with my close group of friends or camping with our family, I could be found zipping through a fresh stack of paperbacks from the library. After I begged my parents to put me in competitive soccer around age fourteen, I had less free time, but I still found a way to do the things I enjoyed in between games and on the way to tournaments. I never really remember my mind being still. Even if I was sitting, I was always doing or dreaming up *something*.

The whole nerd factor and competitive soccer thing ended up working to my advantage. By the end of my senior year of high school, I had academic and athletic scholarship offers from two pretty impressive schools. One was a full-ride at a Division III school in California and another near full-ride at a Division II university in Idaho.

I wasn't sure which college to pick. My high school counselor asked me what I wanted to do, and my answer came easily. "I want to help people." Whatever I did, no matter my title, I wanted my work to matter. Pretty quickly, I settled on a nursing degree as a good place to start. What better way to help than to be there for those who really needed it.

Because of their nursing program, I accepted the almost full-ride to Northwest Nazarene University, the Division II school in Nampa, Idaho. The classes were challenging, and we played against the best collegiate women's soccer teams in the country. Even though our little college town in the middle of nowhere smelled like burnt syrup (thanks to the nearby sugar factory) and featured cow-tipping as the top back-alley recreational activity for a Saturday night, I was so dang proud of myself for getting in.

I was the first in my family on either side to attend a four-year college, so my immediate and extended loved ones all seemed to think I was going to be somebody. They also seemed to have an opinion of what kind of somebody I should be. By the time I packed up my room at home, I'd had a bunch of conversations with many of the well-meaning adults in my life. I'd listened to them tell me about their crazy lives, their misadventures, and what they wished they had done differently. They also shared what they considered to be the best timeline for me to achieve certain life milestones.

I took all of it to heart and was determined not to relive their mistakes. By the time I made the nine-hour drive to Idaho, I had already laid out a strategic life plan for myself. Room for error or whimsy or miracles was not included, but the recommended boxes were there just waiting to be checked off.

There were a lot of things I wanted to do by a certain age and quite a few other things I didn't want to do until after a certain age. While my family had influenced some of my standards, so had society and probably Hollywood. Somewhere along the way, I'd decided I would be a hard-working, kick-butt career woman who put family on the back burner until the "perfect" time.

First, I would get my bachelor's degree. Then I'd land a job as a nurse and eventually obtain an entry-level position as an assistant on the corporate side of the medical industry, running to get bagels or coffee for a big-shot CEO. Next, after working my tush off for a few years, I'd be discovered because of all my hard work and earn a better position with a cool title. Proving my worth over again, I'd work my way up the ranks in a big city like Los Angeles or New York.

By thirty, I would find myself talking about "my career" and "stock market evaluations" from my corporate corner office where I would help lead the charge to find the cure for some big disease while still visiting patients and making time for the "little guys." All of this hustle would mean I wouldn't have time to fall in love because, duh, I'd be too busy. "I'm focusing on me right now," I pictured myself saying to *all* of the eligible bachelors who would practically be begging to take me out because I *certainly* would have learned by then how to style my hair and do my makeup.

Somewhere in my thirties, I'd be convinced by an attractive man to give in to the idea of dating. He'd also be a nice Christian guy whom my parents would definitely approve of. We would fall in love, get married, live in a condo in the city, and later buy a house in the 'burbs.

We would start *thinking* about children by my thirty-sixth-ish birthday, never mind the data on aging and fertility. Then my dream hubby, who would look a lot like Bradley Cooper, and I would raise three adorable children. We'd have a nice lawn and a modern version of the white picket fence for good measure. Eventually, I would retire from my incredible career so I could do what I always wanted to do: write a book.

It was *the* perfect plan . . . or so I thought.

As I began my freshman year at university, everything seemed to be going swimmingly. Things were going so well, in fact, I was certain they would pan out all the way to the Bradley Cooper stage.

Then everything went sideways.

It was the middle of my first collegiate soccer season, and I had finally earned my spot as a starting player. I was getting phenomenal grades, impressing my professors, and had even turned down a total of one date.

That's when my glands started swelling.

At first that was it, just some swollen glands under my chin. *No biggie.* Then I got a sore throat. Next the pain moved into my neck and down my spine. And then *all* my joints were aching. A day later, I found weird bumps on my shins that hurt like the dickens when I touched them or tried to put on pants. This was a problem—I attended a *Christian* university and they absolutely required pants.

The next twenty-four hours brought a fever so high I was delirious for half the day. Worse still, sores appeared in my mouth and ran all the way down the back of my throat, making swallowing feel as if I was choking on razors. In four days, what started out as a few cold symptoms, turned into something else entirely. I went from feeling completely 100 percent fine, slaying my soccer games and crushing my classes, to feeling like a zombie barely able to stand.

I missed work, practice, and worst of all . . . class. When I finally limped into a walk-in clinic, leaning on a friend from school for support, the doctors were stumped.

First, the clinic insisted I be tested for a battery of STDs, which was entertaining to me at the time because I was about as virginal as they come. (My life plan also included a strict adherence to abstinence before marriage.) Then they tested me for spinal meningitis and other bacterial infections. Next came tests for lupus, Lyme disease, and tuberculosis. Only one test out of dozens came back positive. I still have the scar on my shin from where they cut out one of those bumps to prove it.

Result of the biopsy, you ask? Well, I passed out. But I *also* got a diagnosis: inflammation of the fat layer under the skin, otherwise known as panniculitis. This bit of info wasn't much to go on though as panniculitis is more of a symptom than an illness itself.

"You don't just get panniculitis on its own," the doctor had said, grimacing, probably because he was also still thinking about the barbaric ice-cream-scoop-looking-thing he'd just gouged my leg with. "It's normally a symptom of something worse. I think we need to do more tests."

Weeks turned into months, and my symptoms continued to come and go in waves. Just as they would start to disappear, they would return again, always in the same order: glands, neck pain, joint pain, fever, bumps, mouth sores. As you can imagine, any dreams I had for turning down droves of future eligible bachelors were starting to feel very far-fetched. To make matters worse, even with extremely understanding professors, my straight-A record was dropping. And it wasn't because I was partying. I was falling behind in my classes, and it was completely out of my control. It definitely didn't feel fair because I'd been doing everything right.

"Your dad and I talked about it last night." Mom's voice didn't waver on the other end of the line. "We think it's time for you to see the doctors here. You need to come home."

While I listened politely, I disregarded her suggestion entirely, exercising that "strong will" of mine. "There is absolutely no way. I worked too hard to get this far." For the next week, I ignored my parents' pleas (and their phone calls) as my symptoms hit me with full force yet again.

I tried to push through as another wave of pain, fever, aches, and sores began to wreak havoc. But there is just no powering through something that's running you over. Struggling to make sense of what was happening, I was starting to get a little mad at God for the whole thing. *Aren't You supposed to be protecting me from stuff like this?* I felt so weak and so sick, and my college friends were avoiding me for fear of catching an infectious disease. I looked like a leper. I couldn't blame them, but *ouch.*

Three weeks later, I knew it was time to face facts. I had to drop out.

Pulling all sorts of weird hours, I worked to get my grades back up before I closed out my first semester of college and that chapter in my life. I packed up my dorm room, made the nine hour trip back west across the mountains, and moved in with my parents at the start of what should have been Christmas break.

The doctors in Seattle didn't prove to be much help until they finally prescribed a steady prescription of low-dose steroids, and I saw some improvement. The light at the end of the tunnel made my parents incredibly happy. Aside from the nasty side effects from the meds, after almost a year of constant illness and recovery time, I was *finally* starting to feel better.

Sleeping in my twin bed back across the hall from my little brother and sister where I was surrounded by N'SYNC posters got old, fast. As I slowly improved, I also became restless. *C'mon, God, I've got a plan to get back to!*

By summer, I'd been out of school for almost five months. My symptoms were being somewhat well managed, so I picked up a couple of jobs in the area. First, I started waitressing at a restaurant, and then I picked up graveyard shifts at a nearby coffee stand. A friend from high school who had also "failed to launch" and I signed a lease on an affordable apartment that seemed decent enough. The place was just down the street from the coffee stand where we both worked on Everett Mall Way. It had two bedrooms and access to a "gym," which consisted of three dusty workout machines in a rundown basement with a deadbolt . . . but it got me out of my parents' house. Good enough for me!

When I could find the time, I put those rickety old machines to work, determined to get my strength back. By the time summer quarter came around, I was really ready to get going, so I enrolled at the local community college. By fall quarter, I felt strong enough to try out for the women's soccer team. Not only did I make the team, I was chosen to be team captain. In the span of just a few months, I had gone from being bored in my old bedroom to being busier than I had ever been.

All the crazy was fine by me. I was making up for lost time and bulking up my résumé in the process. Surrounded by mostly new people at work and all new people at school, I kept my mystery illness to myself. I didn't want anyone worrying about me, plus, I seemed to have it *mostly* handled. It wasn't the best idea, but whenever I felt my glands start to swell, I just popped ibuprofen like candy, doubled up on my steroids, and went right on pretending everything was fine.

It was right about there, in the middle of living my life with all the grace of a one-legged chicken, that I almost *didn't* meet Nicholas Jeffrey Magnotti.

"Nick's a Christian, really cute, and really, really sweet! You've *got* to give him a chance, Alyssa!" Robyn's eyes sparkled mischievously. A longtime friend, she had started out as our family babysitter when I was seven years old and now worked at a chiropractor's office where this Nicholas character, who had fallen off a ladder at work, was a patient.

Despite her enthusiasm, I was *very* skeptical.

In high school and into the start of college I'd endured a tumultuous on-again, off-again relationship with a guy who would often dump me. After a few days or weeks or months, he'd predictably come back around, begging for another chance. Because I didn't yet realize my worth and thought being in love with someone meant you must forgive and forget all wrongs, I kept taking him back.

The last straw was when he told me he couldn't wait to marry me, actually proposed, and just a few weeks later dumped me, listing off the things he'd lied to me about since we'd first started dating. Maybe his goal was to make sure I wouldn't take him back the next time? If that was the case, it worked. I told him we were off forever. Still, I felt heartbroken, manipulated, and completely unwanted. After about six months of bawling my face off about it, I decided I didn't need a guy to be happy.

Fresh off that train wreck, I wasn't keen on hopping into another relationship. Plus, I liked my original life plan better; it was much safer. For all I knew, this guy Robyn kept talking about would be just like the last one. I was resolute and determined not to trust the male species ever again—or at least not until I was thirty.

"It's just not going to happen," I said.

But after his chiropractic adjustments, Robyn had kept on telling Nick things about me and showing him pictures of me too.

One day when I was trying to pick the perfect background for my MySpace page (think Facebook but older), up popped a message from Nick asking, "Do you want to hang out?"

I gave Robyn an earful about the whole thing, but she didn't give up. "It could be fun. You have to give the guy a chance!"

By the end of our phone call, I agreed to go on *one* date. But I thought of it as more of a strategic move to get my sweet, ever-loving friend off my back than a date.

I knew from Nick's pictures that he *was* really cute, and Robyn had said he was a Christian. But I decided in advance he was *not* going to be my type. I'd found out he was a club promoter. I didn't know what that meant (I'd never set foot in a club in my life), but I *did* know I didn't need a "bad boy." I needed someone who had real heart and wouldn't ever break mine. What were the chances this random Nick guy would fit the bill? I was sure the chances were zilch.

As an insurance policy, I asked for a favor from my roommate before I left for our first date. "Call me in forty-five. If I say something weird about an emergency with the dishwasher, just roll with it." She laughed, but I was oh so serious.

When Nick walked into the Starbucks that day, everything slowed down around us, like a scene from a movie. Maybe it was because I was nineteen and impressionable and in dire need of a caffeine fix. But it also had to be because he was so dang attractive. He had one of the biggest smiles I had ever seen, a smile that went all the way up to his beautiful, dark-brown eyes that were staring straight into mine.

He was tall and athletic with tousled, thick brown hair and a strong jaw. But what truly held my attention, once I had a chance to collect myself, was something else entirely. He had a way about him, a confidence and presence that put me at ease. When he took my hand to introduce himself, I instantly noticed how warm and strong his hands were. They were calloused, I would later find from working as a car mechanic—his *non-sketchy* day job. *Phew!*

When he asked what I wanted to drink, I stammered my answer. It was hard to focus on account of the way his muscles flexed under his white T-shirt and the easy way he spoke. He was extraordinarily friendly as he attempted to repeat my long, somewhat-complicated coffee order back to the barista behind the counter. Don't blame me; I'm from Seattle. We are known for our coffee! (Well, and our rain, but that's beside the point.)

"So, tell me more about you," Nick said as he handed me my drink. "Robyn said your name is pronounced 'Ah-lee-sah,' right? I've only ever heard that name pronounced 'Ah-liss-ah.' Is there a story behind that?" There was that smile again.

"Ha! Yup, there are a few stories there!" I laughed and said, "I blame my mother 100 percent!" I'd regained my composure and told him about the time I made twenty bucks off my elementary-school music teacher who messed up my name so many times he promised me a quarter every time he mispronounced it.

"Sounds like you're used to people saying it wrong then?"

"Yeah, pretty much," I smiled. "It's never really bothered me, though." It had always just been a part of my life.

"Well... I won't forget," he said, smiling sincerely, his eyes sparkling.

Talking to Nick felt like talking to one of my oldest friends. After only twenty minutes with him, he already seemed more genuine and honest than anyone I had ever met. It was obvious his heart was on his sleeve. From the moment I realized that, I made sure mine was too.

The conversation wandered from what sort of coffee we preferred, to how he got into the nightlife club-promoting business (a college friend of his), to my mysterious illness, to my love for soccer and his love of baseball. I found myself absolutely fascinated with him and the way I felt around him. He was so confident in who he was, and that made it easy for me to just be myself.

As we got deeper into our conversation, we talked about everything from his classes at his community college and my classes at mine, to religion and politics, to how much we both loved our friends. We discussed our past relationships and shared about our parents and our siblings. We got onto our favorite sports teams, the latest music, and our dream careers (his to be a cop and mine to be an author). Our convo somehow zigzagged over to talking about our favorite numbers. His was ten and he was pretty attached to it. It had been on nearly every jersey of his since the first day of Little League.

Nick looked right into my eyes as we spoke, and I looked right back. Other than the butterflies in my stomach that were clearly attempting an escape, I felt perfectly at ease. I remember wondering at one point why in the world this guy was sitting there talking with *me*. He was clearly smart, a hard worker who loved God, was fun to be around, and he was a gorgeous human being. I kept thinking, *Man, I wish I was thirty so I could date the crap out of this guy!*

The conversation flowed . . . and flowed . . . and flowed until we saw the coffee shop employees had already started cleaning up for the night. Ours was the last table that needed to be wiped before they could all go home. We laughed when we realized they had even dimmed the lights and turned the music off. We definitely hadn't caught the hint! When I finally looked away from Nick and apologized for holding them up, I realized my eyes had been locked exclusively on his for hours.

"How are they already closing?" I asked, feeling disoriented as we stepped into the darkness outside. I pulled my phone out of my back pocket for the first time since arriving and saw multiple missed calls from my roommate and from Robyn wanting to know how the date had gone. "It's 10:10! Are you kidding?! It feels like we just got here!" Five hours of conversation and quite a few empty coffee cups later, we had shut the place down.

"It really does," he said, giving me a quick grin. "Ten. See? That number always comes up for me!" When we finally actually said our goodbyes and hugged, I noticed how perfectly we fit together. The top of my head slid like a matching puzzle piece right under his chin. Absolutely no part of me wanted to leave. I didn't want to stop being in his presence.

In fact, I've never really stopped. And I don't think I ever will.

Chapter THREE

I Used to Wish My Life Looked Like a Fairy Tale

APPARENTLY, NICK FELT THE same way about me because we were basically inseparable from that point on. We hung out the very next day and every day after that and were always talking or texting if we weren't together in person. With our crazy work and school schedules, we hung out at weird hours for short spurts of time, but we made sure we *always* saw each other.

Nick and I were strictly friends at first. As time went on, it was exceedingly obvious that our chemistry had us heading for something more.

"When are you guys going to be official?" my roommate asked for the umpteenth time. My other girlfriends had also been pestering me about this—a lot.

"Why aren't you guys dating yet?"

"When are we going to actually meet him?"

When it had been well over a month, they started to get downright antsy. They probably thought I was making him up, but I just wasn't ready. Maybe it was because of my threatened life plan kicking around in the back of my head. Or maybe it was because of the horrendous breakup I hadn't yet forgotten. Whatever it was, I was just fine taking my time.

One day after the lunch shift, I called Nick to see if he wanted to come over. I'd buckled a Styrofoam container full of fried zucchini and a gyro with extra tzatziki sauce into the passenger seat, thinking we could split it. This was an obvious sign that I liked him as more than just a friend—I don't share my food with just *anyone*.

"I'm on my way!" I heard the engine of Nick's souped-up red Volkswagen Jetta start to purr. "I'll be there in a half hour."

When he showed up at the apartment, I'd already changed out of my waitressing uniform into jeans and thrown my hair into a messy bun. I still smelled like garlic bread, but I knew Nick wouldn't mind . . . after all, he was part Italian. We scarfed down our food in a matter of minutes. As I got up to put the garbage in the trash, he playfully reached out to stop me saying, "Oh no you don't!" Pulling me down next to him, he took the containers from my hand and began tickling me mercilessly.

Now we'd joked around before. But other than the occasional friendly tap on the arm or goodbye hug, we'd kept our relationship very much out of the physical zone. Laughing hysterically, I begged him to, "Quit it!" When he finally stopped to let me take a breath, my body relaxed against his. I wiped my eyes and tried to stop smiling.

"I really like you," Nick said unexpectedly. He was looking down at me, staring straight into my eyes. I couldn't believe it. He liked *me*. And it felt like he really *knew me* better than anyone else ever had.

I didn't know what to say. Even if I had, my voice was gone, all caught up somewhere in my chest. I wasn't sure I was ready for this. I mean, this guy was one of the most incredible people I had ever met, but we'd only known each other for six weeks!

As I was trying to sort through the thoughts in my head, Nick leaned in and kissed me.

And that right there, that moment, felt *exactly* like coming home.

From that point on, I did my best to take it slow. I was nineteen years old with a solid decade left until I was "supposed" to fall in love. Holding back entirely hardly worked out for us as we were crazy about each other, but we didn't cross the physical boundaries we'd both individually set long before we met.

Just a month later, we did end up getting "intimate" out of necessity when he saw me in my most vulnerable state—incredibly sick. The meds had been doing their job so well I'd almost forgotten there was anything to worry about.

I'd warned Nick when we first started dating saying, "I used to get sick a lot but not anymore." I was *going* to tell him everything, but I ended up chickening out last minute. Instead, I downplayed my symptoms and purposefully left out the bit about the mouth sores—*gross*! "It's probably just a weird virus or something," I'd concluded with a wave of my hand.

I knew I couldn't hide it forever because when I missed a dose, or even when I took my steroids later than normal, I battled a flare-up. But I was just so afraid Nick would bolt like my last boyfriend did, and I didn't want to give him any reason to leave. I shouldn't have worried. Even when Nick saw me at my worst, which ended up being a lot sooner than I would have liked, he didn't take even a half step in any direction other than mine.

It all started with the infamous first signs of swollen glands and a stiff neck. I took extra anti-inflammatories, upped my steroids, and drank water by the gallon, praying it would do the trick. But as the hours wore into days, I started feeling the sores in my mouth, and I knew I had to tell him.

"Babe, I think I'm getting my sickness again," I said just about twenty-four hours after the first symptoms started to appear. We were sitting on the couch after a long day of school and work. Already I felt like I'd been hit by a motorcycle going sixty . . . and I knew a semi-truck was right behind it.

"How do you know?" he asked.

I painted in some of the details around what I'd told him before. "It always starts the same and then the sores come. They coat my whole mouth, and I can't talk or eat . . . or brush my teeth." I laughed nervously, trying to erase the concerned look off his face. "But it's not *really* that big of a deal. Just don't freak out if I can't hang out for a bit, okay?"

I tried to smile, but that was hard as a new sore was already rubbing up against my teeth.

"Well, if you *do* get sick . . . I'll just take care of you." Nick smiled and swept my hair back from my face.

"No!" I couldn't imagine him seeing me like that. "Umm . . . You *really* wouldn't want to do that. I get really gross. I'll be fine. I probably won't get sick this time anyway. I bet I'm overreacting." I was desperate for that to be true.

The next morning, I woke up feeling like I'd been hit by the truck. The sores had multiplied from three or four to twenty now on the roof of my mouth, under my tongue, and on my gums. The worst part was I knew they were barely getting started.

The night before, Nick had slept on the couch in the living room as he often did when he stayed too late. When he heard me shuffling around early that morning, he knocked on my bedroom door.

"Good morning," he slowly cracked the door, sleepy-eyed and smiling. Then he caught sight of me. "Whoa. Alyssa, are you okay?" He hardly ever called me by my name. Sometimes he called me "babe," but mostly just "love." From the moment I'd become his, Nick using my given name only meant one thing—he was serious.

"I think I just need to lie back down," I mumbled, trying to articulate around the pain and nearly choking on every word.

Nick put the thermometer under my tongue, and as I started to drift back to sleep, I heard him say, "103? I'm calling your mom."

For three more days and nights, Nick stayed at my apartment. He kept my family posted, talked to my doctor, and called my work when I couldn't make it in. He even emailed my teachers and skipped his own classes and work for the first time in years so I wouldn't be alone.

I don't remember much about those three days because my fever was so dang high, and my episodes always caused such intense grogginess. But one moment is etched into my memory forever. My temperature had spiked and the Tylenol was taking too long to lower it, so the doctor on call told Nick he either needed to get me into a cold bath or take me to the ER.

Nick knew I didn't want to go to the hospital because they never had any answers. Besides, I didn't have the money to pay for it. So Nick sweetly and respectfully helped me get down to my underwear and sports bra, cautiously moving around the swollen bumps on my legs. Then he gently lifted me out of bed and carried me to the bathroom where he oh-so-carefully placed me in a bath of cool water.

I cried out in pain as what felt like freezing water touched my burning skin. "I'm so sorry, love," he said with tears in his eyes.

Nick sat next to me, stroking my hair lightly. Tears leaked from the corners of my eyes, in part due to the agony I was in, and on account of the gratefulness I felt for this man whom I'd only known for a handful of months.

Thank you, God. I thought as I drifted into another night of fitful, fever-induced sleep. Nick seemed like an angel, too good for me. Once I was better, I even tried to convince him that he was wasting his potential being with a sick person like me.

But he insisted he had no choice. "I'm yours, love. This is just how it's going to be."

Shortly after my symptoms eased, I got a call at work from my mom saying, "You need to come home immediately. I have something to tell you."

I left work that day thinking someone died. And in a way, after what my parents told me, it felt as if someone had. My parents were getting a divorce.

Deceit and lies were exposed. The dad who I loved going on walks with, building things with in my childhood, who asked me for help when he wanted to start a new crazy project in our backyard, the dad who I looked to for everything and trusted with anything, didn't seem to be who I thought he was.

For a time, my relationship with him would become almost nonexistent. I'd been a daddy's girl as a kid, but I could barely speak to him now. I was incredibly hurt and extremely angry.

The family house was sold, and my family scattered. Dad moved into his best friend's spare bedroom. Mom, the woman who had sit-down dinners ready every night, would end up living in a friend's cabin where the wood-paneled kitchen was just a quarter of the size of her old one.

I struggled to make sense of life without my family intact. The first seeds of mistrust in God took root in my nineteen-year-old heart. First my mystery illness. Now my family was broken. *Why would God allow these things to happen?* I didn't know, and I didn't try too hard to find out. It felt easier to bury the question than try to answer it.

Nick was my rock through it all. He tried to encourage me to mend things with my dad, but I refused because all I felt was anger. With everything going on with my family and the many sides to the story, I began feeling like Nick was the only person I could trust. But even with all the ups and downs we'd already experienced, it felt to me and my thirty-year plan like things were getting too serious too fast.

One night after a somber discussion about my parents' relationship, I gently warned him, half joking, but half not, "You'd better not use the 'L-word' anytime soon." Nick had almost slipped up and said "love" in reference to me, the day before. With everything going down in my family lately, I wasn't even sure I believed in "forever love" anymore. Plus, if I really fell for Nick or even admitted I already had, there'd be no hope for salvaging my life goals. I'd probably end up with a broken heart, if not immediately, then twenty-seven years from now like my parents.

Not too many days later, just as we sat down to takeout from our favorite Thai restaurant, Nick turned to look at me, determined as I'd ever seen him.

"I don't care whether or not you want to hear it," he said, his jaw firmly set. "I love you, Alyssa. I just love you, and that's how it is. I'm not going anywhere no matter what you do or what you say. And I'm going to tell you I love you from here on out."

Startled by his intensity, I couldn't help the happy tears that fell. A million emotions ran through me as I kissed him hard. I couldn't fight it. Plan or no plan, I was completely and irrevocably in love with Nick.

My life might forever be altered, but at that moment, I knew I was right where I was meant to be.

Still, I found myself doing everything in my power to make my old life plan jibe with Nick in it. I worked hard at school and at the restaurant during the day and manned the coffee shop at night. I figured if I worked my tail off, there was no reason I couldn't pull off having a husband *and* achieving all my career goals by the time I was thirty. Plus, we were *both* busy. Nick's schedule and work ethic matched mine with his club-promoting business on top of school and his day job.

The club-promoting business, as I'd found out, was Nick and a few of his buddies getting people out on certain nights to special events. Because their "party boys" team was a group of connected guys, they made good money doing so. I helped by adding my name to their lists and accompanying Nick on club nights whenever I could. Sometimes that was the only way we would get to see each other.

At the clubs, we stayed out of trouble. But Nick's friend and business partner Jay seemingly did the opposite. The two had met in college, quickly becoming friends and going into business together. Nick was excited about the prospect of making extra cash to help save for a future house. Jay had similar goals . . . but he was really enjoying himself while he was at it. Where Nick was the straight-and-narrow guy, standing outside, seldom breaking a rule or putting a toe out of line, Jay was not. The number of drinks his business partner consumed and the new girl on his arm every night quickly earned Jay the slot of my least favorite of Nick's friends.

"Why are you even friends with Jay?" I asked Nick, point-blank, one night after we got back from a promotional event.

Nick's eyebrows shot up in shock and maybe a hint of amusement. I'd always been one to speak my mind, but this must have sounded kind of harsh.

"You guys just seem . . . different." I was full of nineteen-year-old, think-I-know-it-all "wisdom."

"Why am I friends with Jay?" he repeated, as if the answer was obvious.

"Yeah . . . I mean, you guys just seem so opposite." I shrugged my shoulders as casually as I could, trying not to show him just how much distaste I felt for his friend.

"Jay is one of my best friends, and he always will be." Nick held my gaze as he continued, "He is generous, kind, and one of the most loyal guys you will ever meet. He's a *good* guy. God's got a plan. He's working on him." He seemed so sure of it.

Hmm. I didn't see it. "Whatever, babe. It's fine." I let it go, but internally I was still shaking my head.

During the next few months, I didn't ask about Jay much anymore. In fact, I pretty much forgot about the whole thing because the two of them stopped hanging out on a weekly basis. After a shooting broke out just ten feet away from us on the street outside one of the clubs, Nick dissolved his share of the company and took a step back. In the end, he decided all the money in the world wasn't worth the risk.

Without the clubs at night, Nick started visiting me while I was on nightshift at the coffee stand, parking his Jetta by my window for hours to talk as I restocked and cleaned, only moving whenever a customer pulled through.

On a beautiful snowy night in January just six months after we met, Nick got down on his knees behind my childhood home and asked me to marry him. The answer left my lips before he'd even finished asking the question. My "Yes!" echoed happily across the snowy silence as we kissed under the stars.

My family adored Nick, but the second they heard our plans, both sides of our family were asking, "Do you think you're moving too quickly?" My friends, who were delighted when we finally started dating, got cautious once we were so quickly engaged.

Not worrying too much about other people's opinions, we got right down to planning.

"I asked Jay to be a groomsman today," Nick casually mentioned when he got back from seeing his friend one day. Now that they no longer worked together, they'd meet for lunch or baseball games during the week. I didn't care as long as I didn't have to go.

"You what?" I tried to suppress my shock. We'd discussed his other groomsmen choices, and I hadn't batted an eyelash. I liked his other friends.

"Yeah," Nick's smile was big. He had obviously left Jay's name out of the list he'd given me on purpose. "You gotta stop fighting this, Alyssa. He's my friend. He always will be. You might not understand it. But you don't have to." He paused before adding, "God has a big plan for his life, love. Just wait and see."

Why does he have to keep saying that? Inside, I scoffed at Nick's faith. I mean, I believed in God. But I knew He didn't help just *anybody*.

I scowled, trying to stuff down my rage. "There's no chance you can *uninvite* him to be a groomsman, is there?" But seeing his reaction had me wondering for a split second if I'd gone too far.

"Drop it, Alyssa." Nick's voice was stern. The conversation was over.

"Whatever. Just tell him he's not allowed to hit on my friends!"

Nick shook his head, frowning as I continued to grumble.

Eventually I got over it, but that didn't change my disdain for Nick's friend. In fact, I think it made it a little worse. I avoided Jay like the plague in all the events leading up to our big day.

Just one year after we'd met at the Starbucks across from the mall and six months after he proposed, Nick and I were married. We were young and broke and head over heels in love.

We paid for most of the wedding ourselves because after my family's recent upheaval, there wasn't a spare cent to go around on my side. I found an on-sale wedding dress with poufy layers for $200 that my grandma offered to pay for, and a family friend bought us a photography package as a wedding present. Our ceremony and reception were held at my childhood church with our Pastor Eric as the officiant. A few of our around ninety guests were asked to bring food to further cut costs, making it a potluck wedding. Emily Post probably turned over in her grave, but we didn't care; we were just happy to tie the knot.

Oh, and Nick's friend, Jay? He not only attended as one of Nick's groomsmen—he caught my garter.

With our pop-up wedding behind us, we flew off to Nick's mom and stepdad's timeshare in Cabo to spend a week enjoying the sun-soaked sandy beaches and each other. Not even a tropical storm dampened our fun—we just swam in the pool with the wind and rain, laughing and kissing whenever lightning struck. We felt invincible. And for a moment, I think we were.

Chapter FOUR

I Used to Believe I Needed to Control Everything

"HAPPY BIRTHDAY, LOVE," NICK whispered into my ear. It was morning.

"It's my birthday?" I was so tired I didn't open my eyes at first, but I did manage a slight smile. *What have I forgotten? Why am I so groggy? I need coffee.* My heartbeat picked up as I tried to pick my way through the mental fog.

Finally, the haze started to clear. It all came rushing back to me. It was my twenty-fourth birthday. We were in the hospital. Nick was sick.

It was our third morning in a row with no diagnosis. I kept my eyes squeezed shut, wishing it all away. I prayed I would open them to find us in our own bed cozied up under our down comforter. But when I squinted one eye open, no such luck. I was squished into a tiny hospital bed on the fifth floor where the blankets were thin and scratchy. Last week wasn't a dream, it was a real-life nightmare, and I definitely wasn't at home. As reality set in, I felt my eyes brimming with tears.

Then Nick's voice broke through. "This is for you," he said as he held up an envelope and a small square box carefully folded in teal wrapping—one of my favorite colors.

"Oh!" I said, surprised and trying to hold back my tears. "Thank you!"

I hadn't even remembered the date. I definitely didn't expect a gift.

Suddenly, the realization dawned on me that I'd finally done it! For the first time in a very long time, maybe even since our wedding, I hadn't set expectations for how I wanted a big day of ours to go. This is how I should have been living all along.

A twinge of guilt tugged at my awareness as I remembered the words I'd shouted at Nick during the anniversary debacle a month before and the words I'd thought before falling asleep that night.

As I read the personal and carefully written-by-him inscription inside my birthday card, I saw Nick smiling at me out of the corner of my eye. I knew he finally realized just how much his thoughtfulness meant to me.

"Oh, babe . . . you are too sweet," I said, tears now running freely down my cheeks. I kissed him tenderly.

I no longer really cared about my birthday or the cards or gifts. I didn't care about anything—other than him. All I really wanted was to gather up all my strength and combine it with his to fight whatever was threatening his health and our new chance at happily ever after. I wanted this nightmare to go away for good so we could get back to fixing whatever had gone wrong. I wanted my husband back—flaws, forgotten anniversaries, and all.

"Open it, love," he said, nodding at the box in my hands. I could hear the excitement in his voice.

"The perfume I wanted!" I gasped. I'd ripped a sample out of a magazine a month before, rubbing it on my wrist before work. Nick had obviously noticed and somehow gotten a whole bottle of it all wrapped up and to the hospital. I was blown away by him in that moment.

A pang of regret shot through me. How had I equated the materialistic value of gifts to the level of adoration that my husband held or didn't hold for me? How had I spent so much time working for the next raise or promotion over the years but virtually no time working on us? I had been foolish. Naïve. Selfish. How backward I'd had it.

Perched on the edge of Nick's hospital bed as he napped later that day, I knew it was time for a major shift in our relationship. And, it was all going to have to start with me. It was time to get my priorities in check, time to start working toward becoming a better person than I'd been. I'd always demanded the best of myself in school, in sports, and at work. But had I ever demanded the best of myself in my marriage? In the relationship that really counted, was I doing my best? Had I ever fully appreciated the love my husband had shown me the last four years we'd been together? Had I really grasped and held onto the good moments, or had I been too focused on the things that were lacking? Did I try to see him for the wonderful man he really was, or did I just pay attention to the things I wanted to *change*?

I knew the answers to these questions, and I didn't like them one bit. I'd promised my everything to this man and hadn't lived it out. I hadn't really even tried. *This time*, I vowed to myself, *I will give him my best, not just whatever is left over.*

I would love him better, and I would cherish our time together. Because, honestly, the way everyone around here had been acting, I didn't know how much time we had left.

Dear God. I need another chance. Please! God had sure been hearing a lot from me lately. I decided I didn't care. I hadn't asked for much of anything from Him in years.

Later that day, five of my best friends showed up to break me out of the hospital room. Nick hatched the entire plan behind my back so I could go out for my birthday with my friends. First the card, then the perfume, and now this? I was feeling embarrassingly spoiled, and I didn't want to leave him.

The irony of the situation was not lost on me—the contrast between our anniversary a month before and this birthday was clear. I would have rather eaten at a dinky diner with my healthy husband at this point than go anywhere without him.

"We'll just be gone for an hour. Promise," Robyn reassured me. She heard the stress in my voice when I tried to convince everyone to bring me takeout instead. After a few more protests from me, another friend piped up, "The restaurant is just down the street. Besides, you really should get out of here for a while."

"Why? Is my *crazy* showing?" I laughed, but I saw a grimace or two in the group. These were my besties; they were truth-tellers who had been in my life since middle school.

Nick insisted I go. "Maybe it would be good to get some fresh air." I'd barely left the room in days and definitely hadn't set foot outside the building since we'd arrived four days earlier.

"Okay, okay! I'll go! Just give me a second to freshen up." Popping into the bathroom to brush my teeth, I took a quick peek in the mirror. I hadn't washed my face or taken a shower in over forty-eight hours. The black charcoal I'd used to line my eyes was smeared and had me looking like a somewhat puffy, tired panda. I put some water and hand soap on a scratchy paper towel and slowly began to wipe away some of the black.

Then I saw something I hadn't noticed before. My face looked different. My eyes were different. Darker. It didn't matter if I smiled into the mirror or not. The girl that stared back at me looked . . . raw.

I had changed, and I almost didn't recognize myself. The fear I felt was manifesting itself physically.

The second my friends and I started down the hall, even more worry crept into my thoughts. *What if something happens while I'm gone? What if my phone battery dies, and they can't get a hold of me? What if Nick suddenly gets worse?*

I was useless at dinner. My friends asked questions, trying to be supportive and to take my mind off things, but it was hard to focus on ordinary conversation. I couldn't stop thinking about Nick, all the ways I had let him down, and all the work I needed to do to fix the only part I was finally realizing I had power over—my side of "us."

I'd been a control freak for most of my life. I'd loathed group projects as early as first grade. Working my way up to COO of a start-up incubator in Seattle, I had knocked that C-level title off my life plan incredibly early. When my boss there pointed out I needed to work on passing off projects to our team instead of doing them all myself, I realized my tight grip was a real problem. Secretly dubbing myself "the worst delegator ever," I decided it was just the way I was. I couldn't trust other people to do what I thought I could do better.

The energy I was spending trying to control everything in my life at the time could have powered a small country! Working hard to get what I wanted worked for me for a long time. In school, in soccer, in my career: I got what I wanted. As long as I had some control over the variables, I felt I could control the outcome of most situations. Because of my white-knuckle-tight clutch on everything—from what kind of toothpaste we bought at home to the time of morning our monthly newsletter went out in the office—I worried incessantly. For much of my adult life, I struggled to fall asleep at night because I was so busy formulating plans around things that weren't in my control or were never meant to be.

When I really started thinking about it, I realized I hadn't just set high expectations at the office, I'd set high expectations for our marriage. And I didn't only have quotas when it came to anniversaries, I had a whole list of expectations for every other day of the year too.

I had expectations not just for us as a couple, but for Nick too. I knew how I thought he should act and what he should say in almost every situation. While I don't believe having standards is a bad thing, I had definitely taken it too far in areas where it shouldn't have mattered. Even though I didn't always say it out loud, I always thought I knew a better way to get things done.

Walking away from Nick in the hospital that day was a test—and the "controlasaurus" in me failed *hard. S*pending an hour in that restaurant with my best friends on my birthday felt like torture. Because from the restaurant, I had no control. I couldn't see what was happening. I couldn't do anything to fix anything. I could have lived in the moment, let go, and enjoyed my time with my friends, but I couldn't stop worrying about Nick.

Even though I thought I had a pretty good thing going with God at the time, I can see just how flimsy my "relationship" with my Creator really was. I didn't trust Him. It's no wonder because you can't trust somebody you don't know. I hadn't ever really taken the time to get to know Him. Looking back now, it doesn't even feel fair for me to say I even knew Him at all. I hadn't partnered with Him on any of the plans for my life—too afraid He'd color outside the lines and mess everything up.

"What are you guys going to do?" my friend asked me as we finished our meal and got ready to go back. "Will you just stay at the hospital until they figure it out?"

"Oh, I guess. But I think we will be out soon." Mustering up the best smile I could, I tried to look confident.

My outlook might have looked like strong faith to others. At the time, I may have even believed it *was* strong faith. In reality, it was anything but; I trusted God only enough to ask if He would take care of the small things. I often forgot to thank Him when things went right, and I was quick to blame Him when things went horribly wrong. I'm not sure where I'd gotten this perception that God was somehow a cross between my own personal fairy godmother and a punching bag. But that's where I was.

Nick and I had talked about this hospital stay being a new start, our next chance. But he was still in there. Things weren't looking great. I didn't know then that God was already working to weave a new start right into the fabric of what was meant for destruction. Our new beginning was a gift I didn't recognize at first because it came wrapped up in a series of horrible days.

I'd asked for change, and that is absolutely what I got.

I'm not saying God made Nick sick. I don't believe that at all. But I do believe He knew what was coming for us and had begun moving all of the pieces of the puzzle together for our eventual good in an unconventional answer to my prayer.

When we finally got back to the hospital, I sat on the edge of Nick's bed and took his warm, familiar hand in mine, now calloused from his work in our yard back home.

"What is it, love?" he smiled back at me.

"I just . . . I feel like I've really messed up," I said as a tear slipped down my cheek. "And I don't know what's going on exactly, but I know I'm supposed to learn something from all this. I think I'm just realizing what a great thing we have. I know I haven't done the best job of appreciating you or us recently."

I didn't know just how many lessons God would eventually teach me through this misadventure, but I knew something big was happening in my heart.

Nick's eyes were soft and playful, forgiving and open. "Me either, love. The second we bust out of this place, we get back to regular date nights and start talking like this more and working less. Deal?"

"Deal." I smiled and settled down next to him on the bed.

He squeezed my hand firmly three times to say "I love you."

I squeezed back four times to say "I love you too," then added, "Forever and a day."

"Forever and a day, birthday girl," he echoed back, running his hand along my arm and up to the nape of my neck, where he ran his fingers through my hair until we both finally fell asleep, tangled up and utterly exhausted.

Chapter FIVE

I Used to Think
It Was All My Fault

THE NEXT DAY A nurse came in bright and early to get Nick's signature. Not to discharge him from the hospital as I hoped, but because they wanted to do exploratory surgery, which seemed to be the only viable option. I didn't love it, but this would be our chance to figure out what was causing Nick's pain and why his appendix burst in the first place.

Life felt as if it had been passing in slow motion for days, but the moment the decision was made to do surgery, everything started rushing by again. Nick and I spent what felt like a second with the surgeon, going over everything that was about to happen. We heard a ton of medical jargon, a long list of all the possible findings, and an honest confession that the doctor still had no idea what he was about to find. Before I had a chance to catch my breath, we were in the prep room with the nurses getting Nick ready for the OR.

"He's so young and healthy, I wouldn't worry if I were you," the doctor said, looking at me and smiling politely before he left Nick's side to scrub in. I couldn't think of what to say. My heart felt like it might beat right out of my chest.

"You're going to have to let him go now," the prep nurse said with a look of sympathy in her eyes. I could tell she meant business because she had a job to do, but I still sort of wanted to punch her.

I knew I needed to leave so they could start anesthesia, but my actions were being dictated by my heart, and my heart was so bound up with Nick's that I couldn't bring my feet to move.

"Are you scared?" My voice wavered as I asked Nick the very question I hoped he wouldn't ask me.

"No, I'm really not." That smile of his was still so confident and sure.

I took a shaky breath and tried to swallow the lump that was lodged in my throat.

"It's okay, love." Nick held my hand and rubbed my back gently as I leaned over to give him one last hug.

I felt like I still had so much to say, but there wasn't time to say it.

"God's with us. It's going to be okay." Nick gave my hand three firm squeezes. He was so strong. "Forever and a day, love . . . I'll see you soon."

Tears started to stream down my cheeks. I hated facing the unknown. I wasn't sure what was going to happen next, and I wasn't sure I could handle finding out.

"Don't cry again. You already look tired," Nick said, winking playfully. He was always trying to make me laugh. But in that moment, it wasn't funny. It just reminded me, once again, he was my better half in so many ways. *How had I ever taken him for granted?*

"Okay." My voice sounded a lot stronger than I felt, as if it belonged to someone else entirely. "I love you too, babe." I focused all my energy on the task at hand, which was simply letting go of his. One finger at a time, I pulled away. It felt like I was lifting a hundred pounds with every tiny movement.

The second I let go entirely, a young male nurse wheeled him away, striking up a conversation about cafeteria food, no doubt trying to keep Nick's mind off what was about to happen. He didn't know Nick's faith was as solid as a rock. The anxiety in the room was firmly planted in my corner.

With Nick no longer in sight, I started back down the hall, determined to do *something* to keep more tears from falling. Whipping my phone out of my back pocket as I walked toward our room, I texted a few friends and our family to update them on Nick's current status. Then I focused all my energy on gathering our things. Nick's recovery room would not be on the oncology floor where we had arbitrarily ended up.

I tried not to think as I got into the elevator with my hands full. But by the time the elevator doors opened again two floors down, I was on the verge of a breakdown. I knew the waiting room was just around the corner. Determined to keep it together, I straightened up and plowed forward. Suddenly, our bags felt about a hundred times heavier, and I paused in the empty hallway to lean my back against the wall. I needed a rest. I hadn't noticed anyone in the hallway before, but the same nurse from the prep room earlier suddenly came into focus. She must have seen something in my face because she walked straight for me.

As she neared, she opened her arms, and I about fell into her embrace, torrents of sobs escaping me. I bawled into her scrubs, my shoulders shaking. She was a stranger, but that hug helped me more than she will ever know.

"Don't worry, honey. He will be fine. He's so young and strong. It's going to be okay," she said, patting my back as I tried to calm myself.

I nodded, but I wasn't so sure. Everyone kept telling me he would be okay, but they didn't *really* know. And why did I have this horrible feeling in the pit of my stomach? Something felt wrong. *Horribly* wrong.

Once I had somewhat collected myself, the nurse led me the rest of the way to where my mom, Nick's family, and at least a dozen other familiar faces were waiting. I hadn't texted half of them but word travels quickly when you are so deeply loved by so many. My chest constricted with each and every embrace. It was an encouragement to see so many loved ones gathered, but it also made me feel heavier. I guess I felt like I had to be even stronger when they all looked just as worried as I felt.

Tears were threatening to pull a Niagara Falls again. So I dropped my stuff in a chair and muttered something about needing a snack (though for the first time in my life my appetite was nonexistent). The second I was out of sight, I sprinted to the nearest bathroom, locked the door behind me, and collapsed into it. Staring at my phone through my tears, I fumbled my way to my contact list. My fingers were trembling, and I had to focus hard to hit the right name.

My dad had texted me from work that morning asking if he should come to the hospital to be with us. I didn't even have to think about my response. I'd texted back, "Thank you, but that's not necessary."

"Hi, Pumpkin. How's it going? Has the surgery started?" My father's voice was hopeful but guarded on the other end. He wasn't used to hearing from me since I'd all but cut him from my life after he and my mom divorced.

I wouldn't have called my dad for much of anything at this point, but a few nights before as we lay in that hospital bed, Nick had urged me to fix things with him. "You're going to need your dad," he said.

Locked in that bathroom, I was more scared than I'd ever been. I needed protecting. I needed help. Nick had been right—I needed my dad.

"They took him back. I don't know what's going to happen. They said there's a slight chance it could be cancer! I am so scared, Dad! Something is wrong. I can feel it."

"Calm down and try again, please. I couldn't understand a word you said." My dad wasn't hard of hearing; it's just that I was doing more crying than talking.

I repeated everything, this time trying my best to hold back the tears so I could communicate. I spoke slower, still choked up, but got the point across. When I was finally finished, my dad uttered words I will never forget.

"He's going to be okay, Alyssa." His voice was sure and strong, reminding me of all the times he'd comforted me as a kid when I'd fallen down or scraped my knee. "No matter what. Even if it *is* something bad like cancer, he is going to be okay. You. Will. Be. Okay."

I took a big breath and let it out slowly and told my heart it had to be true. Somehow, someway, it would all work out. For now, I would make myself believe it.

Nagging thoughts still pressed as I went back to the waiting room. If it *was* cancer, how would God take care of us? My doubts countered my faith as I sat with our friends and family, anxiously waiting for news.

As the surgeon approached the glass waiting room door hours later, I immediately stood up. His mouth turned upward slightly as he strode in, but his face didn't give anything away. Was that a relieved smile or a grimace?

Standing right in front of me, he shook my hand and asked if I wanted to go in another room. "That's all right," I said. Whatever he needed to say, I couldn't wait another moment to hear it. Our friends and family came in close as the doctor started by saying he'd been removing appendixes for almost twenty years.

Why is he telling us this? Get to it!

Then the kicker. "I've never, in the thousands of surgeries I've done, seen anything like this."

Oh.

"I don't think it's cancer," he concluded, "but I'm not sure *what* it is."

The two-and-a-half-hour surgery confirmed Nick's appendix *had* ruptured but not from a common infection like appendicitis. Instead, a tumor had formed inside the organ causing it to swell and burst from the strain. Like an alien invader, the tumor had then leaked enough of a mucus-like substance to create a form the size of a large cantaloupe in his lower abdomen. The unique consistency of the jelly-like mass made it invisible to the scans he'd undergone. Along with this new information, the surgeon said he had retrieved a sample of the mass for testing.

"It could very easily be benign. Meaning, not cancerous," he said slowly. "I would actually bet it's benign at this point."

Relief flooded over me to know the doctor didn't think it was the dreaded C-word. But I pictured a mass the size of a cantaloupe in Nick's abdomen and felt sick to my stomach. Suddenly, it felt like everything around me was moving slowly and disjointedly; the people standing near me felt miles and miles away. I tried to hold my composure as new questions began to form. *How did we not know there had basically been a bowling ball in my husband's stomach?*

From somewhere seemingly far off, the surgeon was saying, "We're sending the cells to pathology to get a clear diagnosis. Nick will need to stay in the hospital for at least a few more days to recover.

"Just to warn you," the surgeon said, speaking a little quieter and directly to me now. "We started with just a two-inch incision. But we were trying to get around the whole mass, and it was just so large that we had to keep cutting. The scar will be big, about seven inches long . . . a horizontal line across his lower abdomen like a C-section."

One of Nick's buddies nearby chuckled, but I didn't crack a smile. My face was frozen. *I* felt frozen.

After the doctor had gone, promising to check on Nick later that day, I took a deep breath and turned to our not-so-little-anymore group. Nick's mom was directly in front of me, visibly shaken. I recognized the same wounded look in her eyes that I had seen in mine the day before. She looked like someone who had just been punched in the gut.

"What if it *is* cancer?" she whispered breathlessly into my ear as we hugged.

"There's no way," I countered, confidently. And then quieter still, I echoed my dad's words, "And even if it is, it will be okay."

I was trying to exercise my faith muscle and didn't know what else to say. Plus, I reasoned being okay meant it would *not* be cancer. Then I thought about the two words *even if.* Even if it was . . . he would be quickly healed. *Boom! That's it! Everything's going to be okay! That's what faith is anyway, right? Positive thinking and all that?* I wasn't quite sure, but I decided to hang on to those positive vibes as I waited eagerly for a nurse to tell me I could see my husband again.

A day or two after surgery, Nick demonstrated his relative health to the medical team by proving he could poop, and we were told he would finally be discharged from the hospital.

Later on, our friends got him a shirt that said, "I pooped today!" and we used that comic relief to our advantage, giggling all day long. We let ourselves find it wildly amusing that something like a bowel movement could be cause for celebration, but it really could!

On a more serious note, Nick's hospital stay served as a reminder of the many things about our health we take for granted until they stop working—like my autoimmune disease that still flared up when I didn't pay attention to keeping it under control. Eventually, instead of worrying so much about what didn't work right, I started counting everything as a blessing when it *did* work correctly. I found myself smiling at the miracle that was simply being able to use a toilet.

Before we left, Nick's surgeon came to see us one last time. I noticed his discomfort as soon as he entered the room. "Normally we would have results of the biopsy back by now," he said. "Sometimes we get them within a couple of hours or days at the most. But we couldn't get a clear diagnosis in-house. So we sent the samples on to the more robust lab at the main campus. They couldn't identify it either, so we forwarded them to a few other labs in Seattle, and even *they* weren't sure." The surgeon frowned. "It's, well, very rare that we have to do this, but last night we overnighted the biopsy to a very high-tech lab in Utah where they deal with more unique cases. Unfortunately, I can't tell you how long this will take. I promise I'll call you as soon as I know anything. I'm sorry, guys."

Nick and I locked eyes, but I wasn't surprised with our recent track record. I had almost come to expect vague nonanswers. Armed with only a prescription for some meds and Nick's taped-up battle scar, we were released back into the real world. Only five nights and six days had passed, but it felt like we were walking out into an entirely different universe.

When we arrived back home, our dogs practically knocked me over in their excitement as I tried to block Nick's stomach from their well-meaning paws. Everything looked the same at home. It smelled the same. But it all felt *very* different.

I'd experienced a massive shift in perspective. Instead of walking in like I used to and immediately seeing everything I wanted to change about the place, I saw everything I could be grateful for. It was so good to be home.

As the days passed and Nick recovered, I was still shaken but finding it easier to assume the worst had passed. His incision looked a little better every day, and he was as positive as ever. The further away we got from the surgery, the easier it was to believe this had all been some sort of weird infection. And the doctor *had* said, whatever it was, he had removed *all* of it.

Early one morning, five long days after we'd been released, Nick's phone rang loud and shrill. We'd gotten other phone calls that week, but somehow, this time we both knew exactly who was on the other end of the line. This was the call we had been waiting for.

Nick stood up from the couch and faced me. I crossed the kitchen and wrapped my arms tightly around him with still wet hands from loading the dishwasher.

Those five days at home had only sharpened the epiphany I'd had in the hospital. I loved this man more than life itself, and I would do anything to keep him safe. I would do anything to make him feel better, just as he had done for me when I got really sick right after we'd met. No matter what happened, I was ready to love him with all I had.

My head was right up under his chin, my face against his warm chest, tucked right there in the place where I belonged. I felt his heartbeat quicken. Glancing down at me, he took a deep breath and tapped the green button, finally accepting the incoming call. Whatever was coming, we had no choice but to be there to meet it.

"Hello. This is Nick."

As I heard the surgeon's voice on the other end, everything seemed to shift back into that crazy slow-motion gear. This was it. We would finally know what caused Nick's pain for over a week and what had put him in the hospital for almost the same length of time. We would know if this battle was over or if it had hardly begun. I inched up on my tiptoes to get my ear next to the speaker, my forehead brushing against the scruff of Nick's cheek.

My mind raced ahead in the conversation as I tried to will the doctor to speak the words I wanted to hear. *You have nothing to worry about! It's a benign cyst. An easily-dealt-with infection. A rare-but-removable parasite.* It would make for a good story to tell later on. We would be done with it. We would whoop and holler today, go out to dinner tomorrow with our families to celebrate, and then go on to live long, full lives with a newfound appreciation for life and each other.

"Nick, I've never seen anything like this before. I've never, in all my years, encountered something like the jelly-like mucous you had. That's why we couldn't see it on the scan. It was so fluid-like and sticky. Anyway, that's why the lab results took so long. It was so unusual. I'm sorry it took a while . . ."

The doctor cleared his throat and paused.

Nick hadn't said a word. I wanted to scream, "Get to the point, dude! You already told us all that!"

"Nick," the surgeon started again. "I'm so sorry, but it is cancer. The mass, all the mucus, all of it . . . is cancerous. It's called mucinous adenocarcinoma, a form of appendix cancer. It originated in your appendix but spread when it burst. The jelly-like mass is pseudomyxoma peritonea, also called PMP. I had to read up on it before I called you. I've never even heard of it except maybe a long time ago in medical school." He cleared his throat and said, "It's really rare. I'm so sorry."

"What does all of that mean?" Nick's eyes were wide, his voice quieter than usual.

"I don't know. Honestly, I don't know. I've set up an appointment for you with an oncologist on Tuesday. You'll have to get more information from him then. Again, I am so sorry, Nick."

"Yeah, it's okay. Thank you." Nick hung up with his thumb and his phone dropped swiftly out of his hand and landed on the floor with a thud. He reached both arms around me and wrapped me up tight, holding me close as we collapsed to the floor.

"It's . . . cancer?" My voice was barely a whisper. My breathing sounded ragged.

"Yeah. But we don't know how bad it is yet, love," Nick was already talking me off the ledge. "Maybe it's not that bad? We'll find out."

"It sounded *bad* . . ." I was physically trembling in fear. A rush of cries escaped me and tears ran in rivers down my face.

"It'll be okay. Let's not worry about it until we have to cross that bridge," he said, his voice shaking a little. He rubbed my back and wiped away the tears from my cheeks as quickly as he could while a solitary tear slipped down his own. "We'll get more information on Tuesday."

It was Friday. More waiting loomed in our future. It took all of my focus to just keep breathing.

He kissed my lips softly. "I love you, Alyssa."

"I love you too." My words were garbled and thick.

Why did he have to say my name? Why did this have to be serious? Why him? *Why us?*

We spent another hour tangled up like that. My sobs shook my body as we held each other tight, not uttering another word.

Chapter SIX

I Used to Wonder if God Was Really on My Side

I DIDN'T HAVE MANY words on the day of diagnosis, but the next day I had plenty.

Just a few months prior, I'd launched my own website, a blog dedicated to musings on various topics in start-up culture. I had only written a couple of posts at that point, so when Nick suggested we also use the blog as a way to keep friends and family updated, I was all for it. Not too far in the future, writing for our blog would become my therapy.

Our forever had been altered by that one phone call. In one split second, everything had changed. For such a tiny word, "cancer" sure struck a mighty blow. It left behind a torrent of hushed conversations and a wake of quiet chaos. As our Tuesday morning appointment approached, I decided I wasn't going to let one little word get the best of us. I knew God was bigger than a cantaloupe-sized tumor. And while

I wasn't sure if God was really watching out for us, I made sure I would be more than prepared myself. Whatever it took to get Nick healthy again, I already considered it done.

I read dozens of blog posts and articles about cancer survivors. It didn't take me long to subconsciously decide I would steer clear of Nick's particular brand of disease because, from what I could tell, those stories didn't seem to end well. *Tons* of people beat cancer in general, though. If they could do it, Nick could too. We would beat this and remake the happy life I knew was possible for us.

Four years after our first kiss on that old leather couch in my apartment, it was finally Tuesday, and we were now seated in the green chairs of a softly lit oncologist's office. It had been two full weeks since I'd first rushed Nick to the ER.

"You have to understand something." The doctor's gaze was steady but held a bit of sorrow.

"These tumors are ridiculously aggressive and incredibly hard to get rid of." He wrung his hands as he spoke.

"Didn't they get it all out during the surgery? The surgeon told us he got it all." I tried to sound confident. "The cancer is gone . . . right?"

"Not necessarily. Imagine a bowl of cooked spaghetti noodles where the noodles represent your insides, like your organs, your intestine, your stomach, et cetera. Then imagine that I stirred an entire jar of creamy, sticky peanut butter in with the noodles. The peanut butter would be Nick's cancer."

"Oh . . ." The word escaped me in a deflated whisper. I tried not to let go of my positive outlook but it was becoming increasingly difficult the longer he spoke.

"Our challenge is that it's practically impossible to get out all of the peanut butter without harming any of the noodles."

"Okay. So what about chemo?" According to my online research, chemo should be able to kill whatever was left. "Can't we do chemo?"

"No. Unfortunately this is different. It's not *in* any organs so it's not connected to his bloodstream." The doctor went on to explain why not one of the traditional cancer treatments would work.

For almost an hour and a half, the oncologist poured out facts and statistics, and I countered with questions upon questions, and questions about my questions, trying to understand.

"How does this cancer originate?"

"Why did Nick get it?"

"Is it hereditary?"

And most importantly, "What. Do. We. Do?"

I didn't like any of the answers he had for us except one: it wasn't hereditary. It was a freak cancer. They didn't know where it came from or how it chose its victims.

Nick was quieter than usual for most of the meeting. He nodded his head occasionally, but that was about it. He looked like a deer caught in the headlights having avoided the research I'd dived into over the weekend.

It really was *a lot* of information, but I was in beast mode. I came here to slay a monster, and it didn't matter to me how big or scary that thing was turning out to be. I would figure it out.

When Nick finally spoke up, it caught me off guard. "So what you're saying is you think this thing is untreatable?"

The doctor nodded gravely.

I felt bad for him, wondering how often he had to give news like this.

"You mentioned there are specialists who treat this disease? I can tell you right now we are going to see a specialist. I'm a fighter," Nick said. He'd gathered his thoughts, and now he sounded as determined as I felt. "I'm not giving up." Nick held his chin high as he spoke.

I internally pumped my fist in the air.

"Good for you." The doctor tried to smile, but he didn't look too convincing. It was written all over his face; he didn't believe we could beat it. "You can try to fight it. But I would advise you to get your things in order first, just in case."

I looked at Nick, startled. He shook his head and rolled his eyes a little. He wasn't believing a word this guy said. So I followed suit. I wouldn't either.

The doctor leafed through the thick folder in his lap and passed us a slip of paper. "Check out the surgeons on this list. Apparently they've had some luck." There were five specialists listed in five different hospitals across the United States, none of them on the West Coast. The oncologist repositioned himself in his chair and looked Nick right in the eye.

"Let me know who you want me to send your charts to, and I'll do it. I'll help however I can. I'm so sorry to deliver such awful news. And I so hope the best for both of you." He seemed to be getting increasingly upset and *that* was scary in itself. Shaking his head, his eyes down, the doctor muttered, "Good God . . . you are both so young . . ." With that, he shook our hands and walked out, slowly closing the door behind him.

Where is our good God anyway? I wondered.

"Well, what now?" I asked Nick, struggling to stay on top of my emotions. We needed to figure out our next step. If I had a plan to hold on to, at least I could work through it, start ticking off the boxes.

"We'll do everything. We'll do anything! I'm not leaving you, Alyssa. This guy doesn't really know anything, you hear me?" Nick sounded convinced. "He said he's only treated two other people with appendix cancer."

"Yeah . . . but he said they both died." My words escaped as a whisper.

Nick didn't miss a beat. "That won't be me. I just turned twenty-five, love! I'm in good shape. I'm healthy. That won't be me! There's nothing to worry about. God's got it. He's got a plan for us through this. I know it." He said it as if it were a matter of fact, kissed me on the forehead, and opened the door, gently guiding me through it with his hand on the small of my back. As we walked out into the cold, his arm wrapped around my shoulders, and my arm wrapped around his waist, our steps fell into perfect sync.

Within a few weeks, we'd successfully scheduled consultations with two of the top doctors on the list. These two doctors were respected by PhDs from all over the world. They knew what they were talking about. They treated hundreds of patients a year and focused solely on pseudomyxoma and its multiple varieties. We'd picked the best two as far as we could tell.

First, we flew east from Seattle to Winston-Salem, North Carolina, to meet a surgeon at Wake Forest University. There we were given more information on a relatively new treatment for jelly-like tumors like Nick's. The doctor had given us more details than we knew what to do with, but he also gave us hope.

He told us of what seemed to be around a dozen of his patients who were living cancer-free almost a full decade after having this procedure done. I sat at rapt attention. These survivors were legends.

By the time we made our way to Omaha, Nebraska a week later to meet with the second specialist, we were quite a bit wiser. We knew the ins and outs of what we were up against. The only option we were given for beating this cancer wasn't going to be easy. The disease was wildly complicated, but at least we still had a chance.

The treatment proposed was as high risk as it was ridiculously intrusive. Its technical term was heated intraoperative peritoneal chemo-therapy (HIPEC), but it was often called by its nickname, MOAS—the "mother of all surgeries."

And it really was. I'd never heard of something so barbaric.

Dr. Loggie, the specialist in Nebraska, explained it as simply as he could. "An eight- to nineteen-inch-long incision will be made from the bottom of the sternum to the pelvic bone. We'll remove each organ one by one and inspect it for tumor cells and then scrape the surface of each organ and the abdominal wall to be sure we get all the cells that could be infected."

"Next, we will fill the abdomen with a heated, sterilized chemotherapy solution that we hope will destroy any cancer cells that might remain. The chemo goes in one tube and out another, delivering fresh chemo to the abdomen for almost two hours. The wound is temporarily sealed during this part of the procedure and when the chemotherapy is complete, the solution is drained, and we stitch you up."

It sounded like something from a sci-fi movie, but Dr. Loggie had done it many times. We could tell he knew the process like the back of his hand.

Dr. Loggie said, "I can't promise you guys anything, but I see it as your only hope, and it's a good hope. We've had many people come out of this and go on to live cancer-free lives. Some have made it ten years without recurrence, and that's as long as this surgery has existed," he said, confirming what we heard before.

By the end of both appointments, we were made aware people had died on MOAS tables before, but we didn't worry for a second. If this was what it took to kick cancer's butt and get our lives back on track, Nick would not just survive it, he would thrive through it.

"No question. I want to work with Loggie." Nick seemed so sure of his choice as we flew back home, the glow of the setting sun reflected in his eyes. Finally, everything was feeling a little brighter than it had before.

We booked the surgery as soon as we landed. Asking for their soonest available slot, we were informed Nick would need two more full weeks to heal from exploratory surgery before they could go in again. We got it scheduled before we'd even collected our luggage. Nick was slated to fly back to Omaha to be "carved" open and "roasted" in chemo at 9 a.m. on the day before Thanksgiving. Once home, I wrote "KICK CANCER'S ASS!" in red sharpie over the November 22, 2011 square on our refrigerator calendar. I wasn't usually one for swearing, but I couldn't think of any alternative words that had the appropriate amount of fight in them.

When I alerted our online community of the impending surgery, support poured in. Soon, I saw my posts being shared and prayers started landing in God's inbox from people we had never even met.

The next three weeks passed by in a blur. Nick was still weak from surgery as he recovered from travel. He needed rest, but according to Dr. Loggie, he also needed to get his blood flowing, so we went on walks every day and aimed to get battle-ready. The mother of all surgeries was coming, and we had to be prepared.

While Nick napped and conserved his energy, I spent hours on the phone holding for insurance companies. Pretty quickly, my insurance rep warned me they weren't going to be able to cover the $300,000 surgery. They would only pay for approved FDA procedures. And Nick's cancer was so rare, an approved protocol didn't even exist. I would eventually fight them on this, but in the meantime, our community stepped up in big ways to help us cover the costs. We weren't giving up. And our blog readers and local community didn't think we should either.

Part of the reason I was okay with working so many hours at the start-up incubator was that I truly enjoyed the team I was working with. It wasn't just about the paycheck. The people I got to see on a daily basis were a rare breed of incredible humans. My coworkers were fun and amazingly smart, and our clients were brilliant entrepreneurs filled with belief, determination, and lots of caffeine. Watching them work to bring their dreams to life every day was inspiring.

When my boss, Peter Chee, heard of Nick's impending lifesaving surgery and that our insurance was throwing a giant-sized fit about paying for it, he decided to do something. He and a few others put their heads together behind the scenes to hatch a plan.

They came up with a one-night event scheduled for November 11, 2011. Calling it the Seattle Geek Roast, they would raise money at the Marriott hotel in Redmond, Washington, to "Roast Nick's Cancer." After they explained it to us and asked if we were okay with it, they went to work. Nick and I didn't lift a finger. In the two weeks leading up to the event, the buzz they and over thirty other volunteers created brought so much hype that the Seattle press caught wind. Invitations were posted across blogs and social media accounts and even broadcasted over local news stations like King 5 and radio stations like Spirit 105.3. It seemed like *everyone* was pitching in to spread the word.

Nick and I were even featured on Fox News' live morning show where I naturally talked a mile a minute, sweating profusely, while Nick sat tall and confident, calm as a cucumber. People wanted to know more about the young man whose faith couldn't be shaken, the twenty-five-year-old who wouldn't stop smiling, despite the cards he'd been dealt.

With only two weeks to plan and execute, the event sold out days in advance. I'm not sure if I realized at the time what a miracle that was, but it was. Some 272 tickets were sold but many registered at the door on the night of, pushing the boundaries of the fire safety code. I was in absolute awe that so many people came to lend their support. On the night of the roast, amid talk of cancer, chicken-wing-eating contests, and hilarious bouts of local comedians actually "roasting" local TV personalities, over 130 donated items and experiences were auctioned off. The very presence of so many in our community told us they had our back. And the $50,000 raised blew us away. That one night proved it for me: when good people come together, great things happen.

Just two and a half weeks later, we were touching back down in Omaha to start preparing for surgery. My eyes were bloodshot from lack of sleep, but they were dry. I didn't worry much about the finances anymore because I knew we had an army behind us, and for that I was immensely thankful. But I was still definitely in survival mode—plus I don't think I had any tears left to cry.

On the day of his big surgery, we woke up without an alarm. Glancing at the clock, I noted the time: 5:25 a.m.

"Good morning, love," Nick said as he stirred awake. Squeezing me close, he kissed my forehead, then gently pushed my hair away from my eyes.

We were squished together in yet another hospital bed. The nurses had wheeled in a cot for me the night before but I'd stayed right by Nick's side. I soaked it up, knowing he wouldn't be in any shape to cuddle for a while.

"Jesus, be with us today," Nick prayed aloud. I bowed my head with him and prayed my own prayer: wisdom for the surgeons, a long life for Nick, and faith for me.

"Okay, lovebirds . . . it's time for the drugs."

I sat up a little when a couple of nurses gathered around the bed. *I guess they really did mean prep was at 5:30 sharp.* I looked over at Nick and found his eyes already locked on mine. *Ah, this guy!* He looked so incredible. So healthy. So good. *How is it possible he has cancer?*

Nick's hands were still around me as I leaned into him. We didn't care that there were two pairs of eyes on us. We would say a proper goodbye. He told me, "I love you, and I'll see you soon. Don't worry. God's got it."

I kissed him, wetter than I intended thanks to my tears. Hopping off the bed, I took two steps away before turning back around for another quick kiss. Nick flashed that genuine smile of his. It was so big I couldn't help but smile back.

My stomach ached, and I was shaking, but the confident curve of his lips comforted my soul. Not once during the nine-hour wait would I tear up again.

I pleaded with God as I sat in yet another waiting room. "Make him okay. Make him okay. Make him okay." I whispered my prayer-mantra over and over again, seated next to a few of our family members who'd flown in for support. I spent all nine of those hours willing the doctors to come into that room and announce Nick was cancer-free.

"He did terrific! We got every single cancer cell we could see and ran the heated chemo through just like we planned." Holly, Dr. Loggie's assistant, was practically bouncing with excitement and smiling from ear to ear. "We will do checkups every six months, but things are looking really good for Nick. We don't expect to see him back any time soon."

An hour later I was finally at my husband's side.

Nick's eyelids fluttered open for just a moment. "How'd it go?" His voice was deep as if he'd been sleeping for days. I hadn't told him yet, but he looked happy, like he already knew. Before I could utter a single word, he was asleep again, and my tears came rushing, but this time they were tears of overwhelming joy. My wish, my prayers, my pleas—my best-case scenario had finally come true!

Even though he was sleeping, I said it aloud and triumphantly, loving the way the words felt as they left my lips, "Babe, we did it! Your cancer is *gone!*"

Chapter SEVEN

I Used to Have My Priorities Backward

SIX MONTHS AFTER SURGERY, it felt like everything was falling back into place. At his midyear checkup, Holly told us Nick's scans and blood tests were normal. "Your tumor markers look like those of someone who has never even had cancer. Congratulations, you two!"

To celebrate the good news, we took a week of vacation time that our employers were nice enough to grant us and flew straight from Omaha, Nebraska to Oahu, Hawaii. We planned the trip in advance, believing with all our hearts that the outcome of our appointment would be nothing but good news. We wanted to spend a week on the island, and dang it, we were done putting off the things we wanted to do just because they weren't the most practical. We hadn't taken a vacation since our honeymoon almost four years earlier because we'd been working so hard. We needed this.

Our relationship had morphed during those six months while Nick healed, not back to what it used to be and not quite as intense during those months of battle, but into something that was so much better than ever before. We'd received a new lease on our love and our lives and didn't want to let it go to waste. We were determined to really *see* each other and rebuild an even stronger relationship.

"I don't ever want to go back to the way things were," I said to Nick as our plane made its way to Hawaii. I was snuggled up next to him as he traced the lines of my palm with his finger.

"I don't either, love," he replied with a hint of regret in his response. I shifted in my seat so I could see his eyes.

"Do you know how often I was thankful we had a big house during this mess? Not once. I was thankful we had a roof and four walls over our heads, I guess. But I didn't once think about how we needed a bigger or better anything . . . you know?"

Nick sighed. "Yeah, same here."

"I didn't even think about work or commissions either, just our friends and family, the *people* in our lives." I stopped and took a deep breath, looking him in the eye. "I've thought about it a lot, babe. And I think I actually want to find a new job. Right now they are letting me work shorter hours, but eventually I'll have to go back to full time. And I don't want to. I love who I work with, but I want to do something with fewer hours. I want to do something that gives me more time with you. I want to *really* live our lives, you know?"

"I know. I don't want to go back to sixty hours a week either. No way. That life was crazy! We barely saw each other. I've been thinking too. I want to start doing what I've always wanted to do!" Nick smiled that high-wattage smile of his. "We can't keep waiting for the right time to do things. There is *never* a right time, you know?"

"*Exactly*!" I squeezed his hand, so glad we were on the same page and so excited to be heading for paradise with my man.

For the first half of our trip, we stayed with two of our close friends, Tiffany and her husband, Josh, who was based on the island with the US Army. With them we ate at the locals' favorite shrimp truck, drank cold beer on the North Shore, perused the farmer's markets, snorkeled at Hanauma Bay, and reveled in the deliciousness of a hamburger on a fresh taro bun.

For the second half of the week, we splurged on a beautiful room at the Hilton in the heart of Honolulu right off Waikiki Beach, just the two of us. Each morning we woke up without an alarm or an agenda and walked over to Starbucks first thing for a fancy cup of coffee. Then we'd venture out in our rented jeep for the day, exploring more of the island, hiking to hidden jungle waterfalls, paddle-boarding in the lagoon, and eating our way through an incredible number of ice-cream-filled crepes.

On our last night, we cuddled up together on the sands of Waikiki, watching fireworks explode across the sky. Nick's arms were wrapped around me as I leaned carefully against his chest. He had finally started to gain some of his weight back and looked *almost* as healthy and strong as he had before the cancer. But his scars, which now resembled an upside-down cross, were still tender to the touch.

"I can't believe we are here," I said, my voice barely above a whisper.

"I know, love. It's incredible." Nick's voice was sure. "God is so good."

After all that had happened in the previous six months, I was in awe of where we were. Nick was okay. He was safe. He was healthy. And we were together in a new sense with our new beginning. Maybe God was looking out for us after all.

Other than his scars, which served as a startling reminder of what he'd endured when he peeled off his shirt, the rest of our vacation was miraculously normal. We were just another young couple vacationing in Hawaii, absolutely in love—and it felt great.

Shortly after we got back, still glowing from our tropical vacation, we sat down to dinner with friends and family at The Cheesecake Factory. After Nick's big surgery, we'd vowed to each other we would celebrate all of our milestones. That definitely included celebrating the crap out of being six months cancer-free!

"This is pretty incredible!" Our friend Sean slung his arms around our shoulders and squeezed us tight. He wore a green "Smile #TeamMagnotti" band around his wrist that Nick's coworkers had created to support us in his fight. "I'm so happy for you both." Always affectionate, he pulled our faces in toward his and planted a quick kiss on each of our cheeks. Tears glistened in his eyes and in ours.

Most everyone at the table, it seemed, teared up a time or two. This dinner truly felt like a miracle. Just eight months before, all of these people were waiting on Nick's dire diagnosis in the waiting room of the hospital just down the street. Here he was fully alive and well in front of us, happily stuffing his face with pasta. Later that night, the servers would deliver a complimentary dessert—with extra whipped cream. Liquid chocolate words were scrawled across the rim of the white plate: "Congrats on 6 months!"

Nick blew out the lit candle on top as we all whooped and hollered. He leaned over and kissed me hard just as I was grabbing a tissue to dab at my eyes.

"You guys," Nick addressed the group smiling. "Just . . . thank you! Thank you for praying for me and for everything you guys did to help me be here today. I couldn't have done it without you. You guys are amazing!"

I thought about how supportive our friends and family had been, about the hundreds in our community near and far who had helped six months earlier, and those whom we'd heard from as I continued to blog. We surely hadn't gotten there on our own. It really did take a village. This time I let the tears fall. Incredible things were happening, and something even better was just around the corner. I could feel it.

Later that week, Nick and I sat at the kitchen table and made a plan for the rest of our year. I would start looking for a different job immediately as we discussed, one that wouldn't require so many hours at the office and that hopefully was a bit closer to home. And Nick? "Po-Po!" We both said simultaneously, cracking up at our timing. Nick had wanted to be a police officer his entire life.

"I want to help people when they are in dark places. Being a cop seems like the perfect job for me because people are in a tough spot on the street or when they're getting arrested, you know?" He'd first told me about his dreams of becoming a public servant back when we were dating, and it was great to hear his excitement as he spoke about it again.

If we put these career changes into effect, we figured we'd make maybe half of what we were used to. But we were determined to live our lives more passionately, with our priorities in check, no matter the sacrifices. Plus, we could sell our too-big-for-us house sooner rather than later to lighten the financial load. "Three cheers for not being house poor!"

There were a few other things that we agreed needed to change, along with our careers.

1. We would start doing weekly date nights.
2. We would get back to going to church regularly (Nick's request).
3. We would keep celebrating . . . *everything*.

4. We would check in with each other daily, making nightly "talk time" a priority.
5. We would start taking vacations and going on adventures *at least* once a year.

We would do all of these things no matter what.

Our trip to Hawaii felt like our first step in the right direction—a first attempt at putting our new life strategy into action, and it had gone famously—so we were determined to keep it up. We knew these happy memories we were making would last forever, which mattered a whole lot more to us than having fancy things. Cancer was giving us the courage to finally throw away the things that didn't truly serve us in exchange for a life of meaning—and we were pumped!

The next few months were a whirlwind as we began hatching our plan to get out of the jobs that we'd let take over our lives. I began talking to my network and putting feelers out, looking for the perfect position, while Nick got serious about getting hired on at a local police department.

As time passed, we still worked diligently but forced ourselves to leave the office as early as possible each day. We made phone calls during our commutes, and I researched and applied for jobs on my lunch breaks. After what felt like forever, I still hadn't found the right fit for me yet, and Nick had encountered a roadblock. He couldn't be considered for hire at *any* police department until he had seven years of cancer remission under his belt.

Nick didn't let this speedbump derail his plan. Instead, he aimed for the closest career he could think of in law enforcement that didn't have any health requirements. By early summer he'd already begun jumping through the hoops to become a bail enforcement officer and had registered for all the tests that eventually secured him his license.

Not too many weeks later, I stood in the bathroom, staring dumb-founded at what I held in my hand. "Babe!" I shouted. Nick rushed into the room, and his eyes went huge when he realized what I was holding.

"You're *pregnant?*" He started to cry as he lifted me up into his arms, spinning me around, his incision almost fully healed. We kissed, weeping tears of joy. We'd thrown to the wind our previous plan to wait to have kids when we realized just how short life could be. But doctors had warned us it could be difficult because of Nick's treatment so we hadn't expected this outcome so soon.

We spent the next few days on cloud nine, talking about names incessantly and excitedly sharing our good news with a select few. Nick even took to talking to my stomach as we lay awake at night discussing plans for our sweet babe. What would she do with her life? What would he look like? Who would she be? I was a tad nervous because we didn't have all our ducks in a row as far as our careers went, but Nick was healthy! We were going to have a baby, and it was going to be glorious!

Then just as quickly as our worlds had turned sunny with the news of an impending bundle of joy, everything flipped again. I started bleeding. After a blood test, our fears were confirmed. We were losing our baby.

Our crazy, incredible joy quickly turned to deep, deep grief. I was devastated. Nick was crushed. Telling our family was the worst. I hurt . . . physically, emotionally, spiritually. *Everything* hurt.

We named our sweet little babe, who I'm convinced was a boy and tried to hold each other up without falling down ourselves. The little life inside me, no matter how small, took a part of me with it once it was gone. I wanted so badly to be back in that blissfully happy place I'd been in before, but it felt like every day was a struggle.

God, You made Nick better. Surely, You could have saved my tiny baby too?

Eventually I found a way to move forward, but it was only by pushing a God I couldn't understand just a little bit further out of the picture.

"Again?" A month later, I couldn't believe I was holding another positive pregnancy test in my hand. I wanted to be happy. I wanted to be hopeful. But instead, I found myself completely overwhelmed.

Falling into Nick's arms, I sobbed uncontrollably as fear gripped my heart. I was traumatized. I wasn't ready for another loss and never wanted to feel that pain again. I couldn't believe this was happening to us! Those last weeks, we'd barely even done anything that *could* get us pregnant.

"Don't cry!" I could hear the joy in Nick's voice. "This is incredible!" I looked up to his face and saw sincere hope and wonder and that scared me even more. This positive test just seemed like a warning of all that could go wrong.

"But what if we lose this one too?" I sobbed into his shirt.

Nick tenderly used both of his hands to lift my tear-filled face to his. He couldn't stop smiling. "God's got it, love. There's a plan." He stroked my hair and said, "It's going to be okay, no matter what. We just have to trust."

I spent the next few months doing just that—or trying, at least. My prayers turned into a chant of sorts. Inhaling and exhaling, I'd repeat: "This baby is strong. This baby is healthy. This baby will be full term."

My doctor had been very clear all along that she didn't have the highest hopes. At first she feared my high hormone levels were just left over from the last pregnancy. "If we are able to see the heartbeat, things will more than likely work out," she'd promised.

The day of our seven-week ultrasound came, and I was nervous as could be. When the clear flutter of a tiny heartbeat finally came into view, the technician smiled. "Congratulations, you two!"

I couldn't believe my eyes. Tears streamed down our cheeks as Nick squeezed my hand, and we gazed in wonder at the little screen. Finally, we would have a happy reason to go to the doctor.

Nick was overjoyed, but I didn't *fully* let myself believe it until we hit the twelve-week mark. Once we were there, I tried to lean into the miracle and pulled out all the stops, told all of our close friends and family, and asked one of my besties to do a little photo shoot. We knew nothing in life was promised, but our sweet little love had made it this far. And this was a milestone worthy of celebration!

A few days later, armed with some incredible pictures and a crazy new hope, we announced our big news online. Everyone was thrilled. The number of people following our blog had grown considerably as I'd publicly journaled through the loss of our first baby. It was incredible to receive so much affirmation and support for our second pregnancy. Our friends near and far had been with us through so much, they were really starting to feel like family.

About a week later, Nick passed his final exam to secure his bail enforcement license. When his badge was ready, you couldn't have done a thing to get the proud grin off of his face. And Nick wasn't just excited about the good things going on, he was making good plans for the bad stuff of our past.

"I really feel like I had cancer for a reason, love. It's like a tool I am supposed to use," Nick said as he sat across from me on the couch. All I could do at first was stare at him with my mouth open as he added, "I want to do something good with it."

How are we going to do that? I wondered. I had no clue how we could turn something so horrible into something good. So I went the first place I always went when I didn't know what to do: Google. I typed "doing good with cancer" or something like that into the search bar, and one of the first links that popped up was about a girl with cancer who was creating good out of her bad.

"Have you ever heard of Austen Everett?"

"I haven't. Why?" Nick asked.

"I just found this girl. She's from Washington, and she's a soccer player. She has lymphoma, and she's started a nonprofit to help kids with cancer. Pretty cool . . . Austen. I've never heard of that name for a girl before."

"Me either. I love it. That's her name." Nick smiled wide.

"Yeah, that's what I said," I smiled back. "Her name is Austen Everett."

"No, I mean that's *her* name." Nick grinned mischievously. He reached over to touch my swollen belly. "That's her name. Our girl."

"Babe. We don't even know if it's a girl," I said, laughing.

"I know. But that's her name." He smiled again, winked, then changed the subject.

I sighed. My husband! I didn't dare get my hopes up for a girl, and here he was already calling the shots and trying to name her too. That man was determined.

I'd finally landed a new job working for one of the fastest-growing tech startups in the Seattle area. I knew one of the founders from my work at the incubator, and the employment package they offered was pretty impressive for a new company. I was more than happy to give up my previous salary and fancy title. Best of all, I would be able to work almost entirely from home.

The execution of our plan to rearrange our priorities was taking shape before our very eyes, and everything was aligning. We were rebuilding a happy marriage and creating a life and careers that mattered to us. Nick and I were no longer bending our values around our work but working our values into the very fabric of our lives. We spent intentional time together every day. We were having a baby! We were putting into action the lessons we'd learned over the previous ten months, and it seemed like we were finally reaping the rewards.

Our new life didn't look *anything* like the life I'd planned for myself as a teenager. That plan hadn't accounted for a husband, a baby, a job where I worked in my pajamas all day, and it definitely had not accounted for cancer. But at the age of twenty-five, I was happier than I'd ever been.

Nick and I often stayed up late into the night, excitedly talking about our future. "I seriously cannot even believe this," Nick said one evening as we were getting ready for bed. "I'm going to be a dad and *kind of* like a police officer! Ha! And I have the best wife a guy could ask for! Seriously, love, I just feel so blessed." His smile was a permanent fixture.

After Nick fell asleep beside me later that night, I talked to God. It had been a while, but I figured He deserved a little gratitude from me.

"God? Umm . . . thank you. I know I don't deserve this. I'm sorry it took me so long, but I see what You've done in us through Nick's getting sick. Thank You for our second chance. Thank You for this second baby. Please keep this one safe in my tummy. Lord, I . . . trust You. Amen."

Even as I prayed, I felt torn. I wanted to believe God was good. I wanted to trust Him. I wanted to believe He was the one to thank for this miracle growing inside me. But wasn't He also the one to blame for our baby dying? I was thanking Him for Nick's health, but this same

God was the one who let him get sick. Those weren't things I could easily forget.

My heart ached with uncertainty, but I pushed it aside yet again. I would figure all this God stuff out later. I didn't have time to worry about it now. I just wanted to be happy. *I needed to be.*

Chapter EIGHT

Then I Realized the Journey Had Just Begun

NICK AND I KEPT up with and enjoyed our new nightly ritual of intentional conversation before bed. One night as we neared my fourth month of pregnancy, we were sitting on the couch eating popcorn during our "talk time," when suddenly, I sensed something was different. It was as if I could feel Nick's energy shift. My mind started racing. "Babe, what's going on?"

He was in the process of drumming up an official bail business partnership with a friend. *Is it something to do with that? Did he quit his job too early? Do we need to sell the house now?* I was trying to work out our finances in my mind when Nick finally spoke up.

"Love, I don't want you to worry but . . . I probably need to call Dr. Loggie tomorrow."

"Uhh . . . why?" My voice was squeaky with surprise. Nick's twelve-month postsurgery follow-up was just over a month out. *What in the world does he need to talk to the doctor about before then?*

He grimaced and said, "It's probably nothing, but my stomach has really been hurting the last few days."

My mouth fell open. He'd *just* had a precautionary colonoscopy a week before, and the results had been perfect. Not a hint of anything anywhere. I pulled my feet off of his lap and scooted closer to him. "What kind of *hurt*? You should have told me!" My hand was on his arm now, and I was sitting on my feet, the bowl of half-eaten popcorn forgotten behind me.

"I don't think it's anything. Probably just something healing up funny."

I tried to keep my face calm as I struggled to process his words.

"I don't want you to worry, love." Nick looked down at his hands as if he regretted bringing it up.

"No, I won't. I'm glad you told me, babe. Don't worry—I won't worry. I promise! We won't cross that bridge unless we have to, right? We can call him in the morning—just to make sure. But . . . you don't think it's . . . back . . . do you?"

"No. Of course not. I'll just call him to be safe. I am *not* worried. I just want to make sure." He gave me a sideways grin and pulled me into his lap. "Now, back to names. We already have a girl's name, but just in case, what about Spartacus for a boy?"

I rolled my eyes and laughed. For the rest of the night, I tried to think only happy thoughts. It didn't work though. Instead, I counted down the hours till morning.

When Dr. Loggie returned Nick's call the next day, he said there *was* a good chance the bloke who'd performed his colonoscopy a week prior had accidentally bumped something to cause the pain. There wasn't anything in the procedural notes, but he assured us that could very well be the case. Nick's pain seemed to ebb and flow. He told the doctor, "It's not that bad." Nevertheless, Loggie advised us to bump up the one-year postsurgery appointment check-up, just to be sure.

After we'd booked the soonest opening available, about five days out, I felt like we were overreacting. *What are we doing flying across the country for a bellyache?* But Nick thought it essential we do what the specialist had asked.

Good thing, too, because as the days wore on, Nick's pain got consistently worse. Three days later as Nick was getting into bed, he suddenly yelled out in pain and curled into the fetal position. After what felt like forever, he was able to tell me it felt like something had snapped in his stomach. I wanted to take him to the hospital right then and there, but he insisted he wanted to try to sleep it off.

"It's probably just a pulled muscle," he assured me.

But after Nick's pain became unbearable, we took a middle-of-the-night trip to the ER. We didn't get any real answers, just a prescription and advice to follow up with Nick's doctor, which we were doing. We were scheduled to leave for his appointment in Nebraska the very next day.

As I drove us to the airport not twelve hours later, I called Dr. Loggie's assistant. "He seems so much worse today," I told Holly quietly as Nick, exhausted, tried to sleep in the passenger seat. "He's in a lot of pain."

"Well, I'm glad we moved his appointment to tomorrow then. I'm sure it's nothing, but get him on the plane, and we will see you guys first thing in the morning, okay? We have a feeling this has to be something from his colonoscopy, but our machines will be the best way to tell."

Just as I was hanging up, Nick asked me to pull over. The second I stopped the car, he opened his door and vomited. He hadn't eaten much, but anything he'd gotten down had now come back up.

My palms started sweating. I could feel myself losing control of the situation, and I didn't like it one bit. We had to get to Omaha fast. I knew Dr. Loggie could figure out what was wrong.

"I'm sorry, love." Nick said, wiping his chin with the napkin I'd fished out of the console. "I must be carsick."

Two more puke stops along the I-5 corridor meant we barely made the flight. As soon as we were seated on the plane, Nick reclined his seat and promptly fell fast asleep. I breathed a half sigh of relief before trying to settle in for what was sure to feel like a very long flight.

Four hours later, we landed in Omaha and went straight to the hospital for scheduled lab work: blood tests first and then a scan on their big fancy imaging machine. Dr. Loggie would review results with us at the appointment first thing the next morning.

That night I wrote a blog post to update everyone on our current situation. I ended it with some thoughts on fear.

I fear for our little one. Worrying about everything every pregnant mama worries about. (Will our baby make it to full term? Will I be a good mom? Will we be able to afford this?) And then I worry about things that most pregnant mommies don't have to worry about. (When and how will we tell our child that her dad had cancer? How well will we be at traveling to appointments like this with a child in tow?)

Sometimes, I lose myself completely. Especially at times like this . . . I think the worst. On the plane today, I was reading from my new favorite mommy book (*The Christian Mama's Guide to Having a Baby* by Erin MacPherson) and ran across this: "Crippling fear is not from the Lord. Instead, it's a tool that Satan uses to pull us away from God's grace. So when you find yourself overtaken by a bout of crippling, ungodly fear, your only recourse is to turn to the Lord and ask Him to fill you with His grace. When my heart was too heavy to pray, I read 2 Corinthians 2:9 over and over: 'My grace is sufficient for you, for My power is made perfect in weakness. My grace is sufficient for you, for My power is made perfect in weakness.'"

Eventually those words sank in, and my fears eased to trust. God's grace truly is sufficient even when you are facing a daunting task like labor and delivery. *Or like seeing your loved one in pain and being unable to help them . . . or both,* I thought. But really, no matter what you are going through or what you are afraid of, those words do apply. God's power is made perfect, completely and infinitely perfect, in our weakness. How amazing is that?

I snapped my MacBook shut that night, thinking through the words I had read and the ones I had just written. If fear was ungodly, then I was corrupt; I'd never been so afraid. What I wrote was as much a reminder for myself as for everyone else.

The next morning, Dr. Loggie entered the room looking well-rested and definitely not panicked. *See,* I told myself, *nothing to worry about!*

"Here's what I'm thinking . . . Maybe a small tear was made in your colon. Septic shock may even be on the way. Which is definitely a serious issue, but we can correct it. Your blood tests don't show any sepsis or infection, and the scan you did yesterday doesn't show anything. But it could just be a slow leak, too early to monitor. To confirm that it is an issue with your colon, I've ordered an exploratory biopsy. Just in case. Ironically, I am getting on a plane to Seattle this morning to speak at a conference, but you guys will be in great hands with Holly. She'll call me with results, and we can make a game plan to get you back to tip-top shape after this hiccup. I am 99 percent sure this is not cancer. It couldn't be. We just did your scans six months ago, and they were perfect. It doesn't come back this fast. Ever. If it is cancer, then . . ." He frowned, his eyes turning dark.

I nodded my head. I got it. Like he said, it wasn't cancer. It couldn't be. We'd already gotten the results from the blood tests and everything looked just *fine.* Nick was still in pain, but it had to be something random just healing up funny.

They brought us to the room where I would wait during the procedure. Nick didn't even have to get fully undressed as the biopsy would be quick. He left his basketball shorts and baseball cap on.

Nick turned to me as I awkwardly tried to tie a hospital gown over his top half and wrapped me up in his strong arms. "I love you, Alyssa, forever and a day. Remember, no matter what happens, we will get through it. God's got this." Then he was gone, strolling out of the room like it was no big deal. He was serious, but he clearly wasn't stressed.

I told myself I didn't need to be either as I waited alone in yet another hospital room.

It wouldn't be long, but I knew I needed to keep myself busy. Too anxious to sit, I paced around the room, reading all the random flyers and eventually found myself doodling on a notepad by the bed.

After ten minutes passed, I grew a bit anxious. When twenty minutes had gone by, something started to feel off. Was there a lineup for biopsies at this hospital or something? They said the procedure would be quick and right down the hall. A small prick with a needle and he'd be casually sauntering back into the room with a new Band-Aid.

When someone knocked on the door, I was sure it was Nick. Confusion washed over me when a short nurse in pink scrubs walked in. "Oh! Hi, hon. It's going to take a little longer." She moved toward the hospital bed as she said, "I'm just here to borrow this." My face must have gone a little pale because she quickly added, "He's *totally* fine!"

"Oh my gosh . . . good!" I exhaled, my shoulders visibly dropping away from my ears. I rubbed my rounded baby belly, still feeling slightly confused at this new information. "Wait. Why do you need the bed? Why is it taking so long?"

"Not a big deal *at all*. It's just that whatever they were trying to remove was too thick to get with a needle." She shrugged. "They're going to put him under and make a small incision to get some of it out," she went on, casually. Uber cool. Chill as a popsicle. "Not a big deal, really. I just need this bed for him so we can bring him back up when he's done."

I muttered a thank you as I struggled to stay standing. She had said "too thick" for a needle? That's what we had experienced the last time when his mucousy tumors were too thick to be drawn up through even the largest gauge needle.

I felt my heartbeat quicken. Alone again, I started shaking my head and began pleading with the Lord out loud. I didn't care if anyone else heard me. I couldn't think of anyone but Nick. "Please, God. Please, God. Oh God! Let him be septic!" I couldn't stop picturing our surgeon's face when he'd said, "If it is cancer . . ."

I prayed and prayed and prayed. I curled my arms around my baby in the hard metal chair in the corner of the room, trying to keep my sanity. I believed with all my might that Nick "simply" had a hole in his colon. I went back and forth between the best- and worst-case scenarios, trying to focus on the scrap of hope I held, but as time went on, I was having an incredibly hard time keeping my composure. I felt like running down the halls screaming Nick's name instead of waiting in that empty room.

Almost an hour later, the nurses finally came back into the room, pushing a bed with my semiconscious husband on it. Going quickly to Nick's side, I grabbed his taped-up hand and moved the sheet back. On the soft skin of his belly, there were four incisions. They obviously hadn't been able to get to the fluid the first three times. *Do they do that for septic patients too?* I wondered. *But, if he was septic, he wouldn't be in here. He would be in emergency surgery.*

The pieces of the puzzle were coming together at an alarming rate.

"What is it? What did they find?" I anxiously shot my questions at the nurses who were still getting everything situated. The one in pink was back, and there was an older woman there too. I'm sure I looked almost frantic as I squeezed Nick's hand, my knuckles white, my other arm around my middle, trying to protect my unborn child.

"It's nothing to worry about, sweetheart," the older nurse responded in a comforting tone and a smile, clearly trying to put me at ease. "They just found some sticky growths. Really nothing to worry about."

The last thread of hope slipped from my grasp. I inhaled sharply and grabbed the side of Nick's bed for support.

"Don't worry." The nurse's confusion was apparent as she rushed to my side. She said it like a question as she made eye contact with the other nurse. "Doctors find stuff like this all the time. It's normally just a benign something or other . . ."

She gestured toward Nick as she put her hand on my back and said something along the lines of, "He is so young and healthy. It's probably nothing."

I suddenly got very dizzy. The room was spinning. I struggled to stay standing and wavered. It felt like I was falling into a very deep, very dark hole as everything around me began to turn black. I couldn't breathe. I started to faint, but someone caught me and eased me into the chair as I collapsed and put my face between my knees. I heard someone saying something over and over again, as if from far off and then I realized that someone was me. "Oh my God, no! God, no! GOD! NO!"

The poor nurse couldn't have known what she said. She hadn't read his chart. She knelt beside me and held me as my shoulders shook, pleading with me to take deep breaths. "You are going to hyperventilate. I need you to calm down for the baby. It's going to be okay."

I couldn't wrap my brain around what was happening. I wanted to run. I wanted to scream. I wanted them to leave me alone with my still-sedated husband so I could cry and pound the walls with my fists. It took me a moment, but I had just about collected myself, for their sake more than mine, when Holly walked in.

Before she had a chance to speak, I saw the color had drained from her face. Her pained expression confirmed my absolute worst fear.

Despite the surgery.

Despite the great results from all the tests.

Despite the fact that he was about to be a father.

And . . . despite *all* of the prayers . . . Nick's cancer was back.

Chapter NINE

Then I Discovered Just Enough Proof

UNFORTUNATELY, NICK'S CANCER WASN'T just back. It was back with a vengeance. There was so much, he wasn't even a candidate for another surgery. As a last-ditch effort to slow the growth of the cancerous cells and to hopefully curb the pain, Nick started systemic chemotherapy. Back home in Seattle, poison dripped slowly through his veins every two weeks.

Not every doctor's visit was hard, though. Each month, we got to see our baby, our light. When my OB-GYN heard Nick's doctors weren't sure if he would make it to my due date, they stepped up in a way I could have never imagined. Their office decided they would do an ultrasound for us on the house every time we came in, so Nick could see our little one as often as possible . . . just in case.

"Do you want to know the gender?" The lab technician smiled gently at Nick and me as she put her hand over the screen. "You're only sixteen weeks, but I can see pretty well right now!"

Our eyes met and we answered, "Yes!" in unison. With so much of our future unsure, I wanted to know as much as I could.

"Congratulations, you two! It's a girl!"

Nick's eyes welled up as he stared at the screen in awe. Our little love *was* a girl. I couldn't believe it and immediately started picturing everything in shades of pink.

As soon as we announced the gender, friends and people we'd met only online sent us all sorts of gifts: thoughtful cards, hand-knit blankets, money for diapers, and tiny shoes for tiny feet. Hundreds more reached out through our blog or social media to tell us they were praying for our family. The generosity once again shown by so many took my breath away. Our little girl was already so very loved.

"How's our little Austyn doing?" Nick hadn't given up on his name choice. Not once. No matter what I said or what other names I suggested we might consider, Nick called our little love, "Austyn." I gave in, only changing the spelling, when I realized there wasn't any other name he would even consider.

"She's good. But I'm a little uncomfortable. Her foot is in my ribs again," I said, groaning a little as I rubbed my aching side.

"I'm sorry, love. The good news is, she'll be here soon," Nick smiled widely and pulled me in for a kiss. That day was a good day, and we took advantage of those as best we could.

Nick and his dad helped me paint her nursery walls gray with a big pink stripe down the middle. I organized all of her clothes, found a basket for her stuffed animals, and prewashed her white sheets with little pink owls on them. We even brought in the spare television from our guest bedroom so Nick could lean back in the rocking chair and watch movies while I prepared. We couldn't wait for our little girl's arrival.

But as her due date inched closer, Nick continued to get worse.

The chemo wasn't just slowing the growth of Nick's cancer cells, it was taking out healthy cells too. His blood counts were down and the side effects were many. By spring, Nick had endured eleven rounds of chemo, and Nick's doctor insisted he take a break from the treatment.

We used this pause to try to manage his symptoms naturally. If only kale juice (or the thousands of other natural remedies suggested) could have cured him.

Nick's cancer was growing at such an alarming pace that the swelling from the jelly made *him* look like the pregnant one. Without chemo, his cancer was growing like a five-alarm fire in the middle of the forest on the driest of summers. Nick told me he could physically feel the tumors pushing against his rib cage and pressing on his organs. The doctors eventually agreed they would have to deal with the low blood counts and the horrible side effects of the chemo because they were better than this level of pain.

Nick was struggling, weak from nausea and dragging from neuropathy (a burning sensation that affected his hands and feet before, during, and after chemotherapy), but he crawled back into the chemo chair again and again.

While things had gone downhill fast, somehow Nick's smile stayed almost permanently intact. His optimism never wavered. His faith throughout these trials, which I shared on our blog as often as I could, baffled hundreds, including me. You never know the depth of a man's character until it's tested. Nick's character had been tested over and over, and it was proving steadfast. His love for God was so apparent, even in the midst of his trials.

Quite the opposite, my heart raged against the God who allowed such agony. My blog reflected many of my uncertainties, but I kept the darkest ones to myself.

"I want you to get better so badly, babe. I don't know what to do," I said one day, feeling utterly defeated. I sat on the floor near the couch where Nick was lying, breathing hard as waves of pain rushed over him. I could barely stand to watch. The nurses had been having a hard time managing his suffering, and it was killing me. I couldn't believe how bad he'd gotten. Not even a year earlier we'd been on a plane to Hawaii, planning our future, amazed at Nick's good health.

I lay my head on his chest, avoiding where his chemo port stuck out at a gnarly angle. As my silent tears fell onto his shirt, I felt crushed. Beaten. Done. It was early morning, and he had been unable to sleep. He'd started sleeping on the couch weeks earlier when our bed stopped providing the support he needed. After almost five years of sharing a bed together, I wasn't resting very well either.

"I don't know how to help anymore." The immense sadness in my voice shocked even me. I could actually hear my pain.

Usually I maintained an illusion of control. But I was starting to feel more helpless than I had ever felt in my entire life. The only thing that came anywhere close to this was my battle with my own mystery illness. But that was so much different. It wasn't this bad. Besides, I never mattered anywhere near this much to myself.

This was my Nick being threatened. He mattered more to me than life itself. He was my best friend. My everything. My only lover. My sweet daughter's daddy. The person I would die for. But we'd tried it all. Every natural and Western regimen we could find. There was nothing left for me to do.

"It's okay, love. I hate that you have to watch this. But I know God has a plan for all of it," Nick said between long pauses, brushing my hair back behind my ear. His hands were still warm but weaker now. "I just *know* it. I trust Him. And He and I . . . and *you*. We aren't done fighting. Our baby girl, our little love, is going to know that God can do *anything*." He smiled weakly but sincerely.

My brain reeled with confusion and exhaustion. *Was this really the world our baby would be coming into?* Nick hadn't eaten in almost twenty-four hours. He wasn't ever hungry anymore. When he *did* eat, it just caused more pain. The doctors had told me this was fine, as long as he was drinking water. There just wasn't much room for food in his stomach those days. Too much pressure. Too much cancer.

"Babe. Is there *anything* I can go and get you?" I asked, hoping something sounded good but not holding my breath.

"Weirdly enough, mustard pretzels sound great right now. But it's too late. Wait until tomorrow."

"No way!" I was so much heavier now because of the baby weight, but I pushed myself up with a smidgeon of newfound energy. It made me so happy to finally have something I could do for him! I pulled on some sweats, rolling them under my large belly and threw on a sweatshirt.

"I'll be right back, babe." I kissed him on the cheek and flipped on the TV to keep him company while I was gone.

"Thanks, love. You're the best wife in the whole world." He smiled again.

I knew I didn't have much time because his appetite never held for long. When I finally made it to the checkout counter at the twenty-four-hour grocery store down the street, the cashier, a woman probably in her mid-thirties, noticed my now almost-nine-months pregnant belly.

"Weird pregnancy cravings, huh? You should have sent your husband!" she said as she eyed my wedding ring and placed the pretzels into a plastic bag. "I remember when I was pregnant, there were so many times I just had my husband go to the store. I mean we *are* growing their children, we deserve to put our feet up, you know?" She smiled as she waited in anticipation for my reply.

"Umm. Yeah," I mumbled, my eyes wide. I grabbed my bag and receipt and hurried toward the door. I didn't know what to say. How would I have explained it? The pretzels weren't even for me. They weren't a pregnancy craving at all. They were a chemo craving. And possibly the only thing my husband would nibble on in the next day or two. In that moment I couldn't even *think* of how to fake a normal reaction.

It hit me on the way back to my car how we never know what another person is going through. I used to assume when people were short with me it was because they were jerks. And that poor cashier probably thought the same about me. I vowed right then and there to let go of any future assumptions about *anyone*. We just never know what invisible mountains people are facing, and we should never assume we do.

By the time I made it back to the house, Nick couldn't even stomach the mustard smell. I wanted him to eat them so badly, I wept over that dumb bag of pretzels.

About a week from our due date, I was always starving because I could no longer eat big meals either. I left the pretzels for Nick though, just in case. I took a few mirror selfies later that morning, intuition telling me our little babe's arrival might be near. My belly was huge, low, and swollen with life. I prayed Nick would be better in time.

Sure enough, twenty-four hours later, five days after one of Nick's chemo treatments, and six days before her predicted due date, I went into labor. It would last for thirty-two hours and put any previous notions I had about labor pains to shame.

When we *finally* made it to the home stretch, I held Nick's hand as I looked into his brown eyes. They were bloodshot, but they were the same eyes I had gazed into over coffee all those years ago. I noticed the way the bones in his cheeks jutted out now, the discoloration of his skin, and the frailty of his hands. But I didn't care. Underneath it all, he was still my Nick.

"Guess what, Alyssa? It's time to push!" the doctor said with a smile. "It's time to meet your baby girl!" Despite my exhaustion, I felt excitement course through my veins. The night had been basically sleepless for me. Our doula, Nick's aunt, had stayed with us to help with the birth.

She was an angel, and I don't know how I would have done it without her because Nick needed his rest.

Like a wave of helping energy, the next contraction mounted to a crest, and I pushed with all my might. Tears squeezed out the corner of my eyes as I regained my breath and tried again. Nick softly stroked my hair, pausing only to tenderly wipe away any tears that fell. He kept his face close. His words kept me going.

"You can do this, love."

"I'm so proud of you."

"You are so strong."

"You've got it, love."

"Keep going!"

Suddenly we could see the top of our baby's fuzzy head in the mirror—the coolest thing in the world and not nearly as weird as I thought it might be.

"How do you feel, Nick?" the doctor asked.

We had indicated in our birth plan that we wanted Nick to hold our baby girl before anyone else, if at all possible.

Nick smiled. "Great!" In all the excitement, his symptoms had basically disappeared.

Adrenaline is a wonderful thing. By my guess, he could have flipped a car in that moment despite his medical state. Catching a baby would be easy.

"Okay then, son. It's your turn." The doctor stepped aside.

Nick moved into position. This was his moment. Our baby and I were one for only a short second more, and then everything in the universe conspired to bring our little girl into this world. With one last push, the first eyes our girl saw were her daddy's.

The joy on Nick's face was priceless as he ever-so-carefully walked our sweet little bundle over to lay her on my chest. The nurses surrounded us, checking her breathing and covering her and me with a fresh blanket, but she never left our arms.

Nick crouched down next to me to get a good look at our girl. She had blue eyes just like mine and strong features just like his. Stretching out all her limbs, she seemed happy to finally have some room. Every beautiful inch of her was painted a lively bright pink. We sobbed tears of joy. She was healthy. She was here. She was ours. We were home.

Six pounds, ten ounces, nineteen inches long. Born March 26, 2013, at 11:14 a.m. to two of the happiest parents on the face of the planet, Austyn Elizabeth was all the proof I needed that true light exists even in the darkest of places.

Chapter TEN

Then I Found the Courage to Face What Was Coming

"OKAY. WHAT'S ONE WORD you would use to describe how you feel right now?" Our camera was balanced on a tripod between us, the recording indicator light blinking red.

My first question was more of an icebreaker to get him talking. I had no idea what word he would choose, but I was thinking something along the lines of "horrible."

"One word?" Nick confirmed, looking back at me.

"Yeah," I nodded.

"Blessed."

I inhaled. His response put me on my heels. *Blessed?* Just the night before, he'd been puking up bits of his intestine, small chunks of tumor, and blood into our kitchen sink. I'd laid my body across his back, trying to somehow absorb the pain as he cried out between each heave. My tears added to the drench of cold sweat on his back. I struggled to comprehend the torment I was witnessing, my faith challenged in every possible way.

I could barely believe his answer. *Blessed?* It made my heart skip. I felt so many emotions in that moment. Two of them I recognized: I felt at least one part wonder and at least two parts anger toward the God I couldn't help but question. I shook my head and moved to the next item scribbled on my page.

"Tell me about when you were first diagnosed."

Austyn was now five months old, growing quickly and full of life. Soon she would be learning to talk and walk. But her dad appeared to be heading toward losing the ability to do both. As I stared down at my questions, the letters started to swim on the page. I didn't know if we would be sharing this with anyone but our daughter when she was old enough. But I knew I had to document as much of Nick as I could, before it was too late.

My husband was still here and somehow still heartbreakingly striking. Hanging out with Nick had always felt like a miracle. Now when I was around him, it felt like watching a universe unfold that I didn't yet know how to comprehend. Something was happening *in* him beyond what I could see.

"Remember, answer these questions like you are talking to someone who doesn't know," I reminded him. I knew Austyn would eventually want to know details from his point of view.

Nick answered, "I was first diagnosed with cancer when I was twenty-four years old. And I was scared. I was, at first. I remember when I had just gotten the phone call. I had just woken up. Alyssa was in the kitchen, and I was in the living room. And I answered the phone, and it was my surgeon, and he tells me I had cancer. Man, talk about getting the wind knocked out of you. That was a hard phone call.

"The chemo has gotten to a point where it's no longer doing what it's supposed to do. Even though I was doing chemo, the pain was getting worse. That's an indication that the cancer is spreading faster than the chemo could kill it. So we've decided to stop chemotherapy just because chemo makes me feel so cruddy. We want to be able to enjoy every single day to its fullest. And when you feel so ill you can't get out of bed, it's hard to do that."

He didn't *want* to stop treatment, but the doctors hadn't given him a choice. The chemo was killing him faster than the cancer would. I took a shaky breath behind the camera and blinked back tears. I hadn't expected I would need to learn the definition of hospice care in my mid-twenties.

"Are you . . . scared?"

"I'm not scared of death. God has given me this peace and this blessing," Nick responded immediately. It was true. He actually still considered it a blessing, and I was still dumbfounded. He never showed any emotion even close to fear.

I, on the other hand, felt dread rush through my veins daily.

"Everyone is dying," Nick continued. "This morning, there are people who are going to get up and go to work and not come home tonight. Their families had no idea. They had no chance to plan for it or set aside videos or birthday cards. Their lives end, and they move on to hopefully heaven and their families' lives continue. So I live everyday with the appreciation for today. I'm not concerned with what tomorrow might bring. We could have a meteor hit the world, and everyone could die. And my cancer would be pointless; it wouldn't be what took me out. And I was so concerned and focused on that, and it wasn't even what took me out."

Nick had brought this point up before, and it helped put things into perspective for me, at least a little bit. The world could very well end before he did. Some nights I had to try very hard not to pray that it would.

I wouldn't have predicted these types of morbid conversations would be a part of our lives after being married for just five years. Not in a million years. But here we were.

Nick kept talking. "I feel blessed because I am living every person's dream. I get to spend every day with the people I love. I get to do anything and everything I want to do. If Alyssa and I want to take little baby Austyn to the aquarium for the day, we can do that. We've been blessed with the time and the means to do that." He smiled wide.

My heart broke again. How much longer would I be able to hold myself together? I needed to get through these questions, but right then I couldn't help but think, *everything?* He was sincere, but had he forgotten that he'd wanted to teach our daughter to play, to speak, to build, to pray, to jump, to fish, to camp, to follow her dreams? *Nick, did you forget you wanted to see our daughter's first steps? Did you forget you wanted to walk her down the aisle?*

I could see the peace in his brown eyes, and I envied his trust in God despite the way things were going. This man had told me, practically from our first month of dating, how badly he wanted to be a dad, how badly he wanted to help people. He now sat in front of me barely able to hold his baby girl. He hadn't even been given the chance to get his business off the ground. His arms were so very weak, just skin and bone. He likely wouldn't even see our daughter's first birthday, and it was ripping me to shreds.

God! Are You watching this? How is this fair?

"The relationship that's developed . . . the amount that I have gotten to *know* God, I just wish everyone could experience it." Nick rubbed his hands together in front of him, his voice cracking. The passion with which he spoke was palpable but so was the physical pain in my heart.

"I just feel so blessed to be up in the middle of the night in pain and be able to talk to God and be inspired to try to help people." He started to cry, his emotions catching up with him. "I just feel lucky that even though I am experiencing this pain, I am getting the opportunity to change lives. I'm getting the opportunity to help people in the Lord's name. Just for me, I hope that they will give it a thought. One day at church, you know, or something. Just one step in the direction. Maybe it's Googling a Bible passage, reading a chunk of something, you know . . . seeing if there is anything that appeals to you in any way, shape, or form."

A few weeks earlier I had asked him, "Do you still think that your cancer is worth it even if you only helped one person because of it?"

I knew what *my* answer was—no! God could find someone else's husband to inspire the droves of people looking for motivation to live a better life. Or God could heal Nick and prove His power to inspire others. Was it worth giving up *my* husband to help other people? It seems selfish, but for me, honestly, it was a hard *no*!

But Nick confidently answered very differently. "Yes. Definitely."

I knew what his last twenty-four hours had looked like. The tumors were physically breaking his body apart from the inside out. The last five months had been hell. The last couple of years had been torturous. All the surgeries. The doctors' appointments. The poking and prodding. The chemo. How was this worth anything? What was the reason for this?

This cannot be a part of God's plan. What reason is good enough? My mind reeled as the sentiments and platitudes of people online and at church swirled inside my head. I'd never seen such incessant, never-ending suffering. *God, please take it all away!*

"Umm." I shook my head, trying to get back on track and clear the memories from that night and all the others like it. It took me a moment to regain my composure. My eyes found the next question.

"Why do you want to do this video?"

"I want to do this video because I feel like we have a good story to share. I feel like we have something special that we can share with people. I feel like God has given us this amazing tool, this 'cancer tool' as I call it, to just help spread love. That's the biggest thing. I want to help people find God and see how great He can be. At the same time, even for people who don't have the same beliefs as me, I hope that you can take what I have to say and pull the positives from it and use it in your everyday life."

Austyn started squirming in my lap; her squishy little body was always so full of energy. I gave her a squeeze and passed her off to Nick. I was in awe of the two of them together. I attempted to focus myself and the camera on the blessing in the middle of all that was broken. I didn't know what the future held, but I had both my people alive there in front of me. Right then, at that exact moment in time, everyone was okay.

"This is my little bug, my little love . . . Austyn Elizabeth. And this is another reason why we are doing this video. Because I want her to know her daddy loved the Lord, and her daddy wants to help people. So she can have the same heart."

"She will." I couldn't help but say it aloud. I knew from the second I laid eyes on our girl that Someone out there had big plans for her life. She was special. Even though things with God had been dicey to say the least, I felt this deep in my soul.

I double-checked the camera was still rolling as Nick continued. "I've just been talking to God about how I know that even if I'm not here, that He's her Father. He's going to take care of her. He's going to protect her. And He's going to watch over her, and He's going to provide for her."

I nodded in understanding, but a fresh wave of grief cascaded over me. I held a tissue to my eyes, trying hard to swallow and not to make a sound. *How will I ever be able to trust God to take care of her, protect her, and watch over her, when that's what He is supposedly doing for you, Nick?*

"I would love to raise her every single year of her life. But every day the Lord gives me with her is just the biggest blessing; just a bigger blessing than I even deserve. Words can't ever describe how it feels to have her as my daughter and be blessed by her. I know that Austyn is going to be taken care of. And I know that the Lord has big plans for her. I know that she is going to accomplish some pretty impressive things in her life. You've got a proud daddy, Austyn. So you're doing good."

I asked more questions about his treatment and the specifics around his cancer. Finally, I had to stop as Nick was getting tired, and I had just about run out of ideas.

When we were all done, we sat together on the couch watching the replay, trying to keep Austyn's curious little hands off of the buttons. Nick had given me the fancy digital camera as a gift a few months back. *A real camera to capture our memories*, he had scrawled in an attached note. I'd cried, partly because I was excited to have something other than my crappy flip phone to take blurry pictures on and partly because I was so upset with myself that I hadn't upgraded sooner.

A couple of minutes later, Nick grimaced. "Sorry, love, can you take her? I really want to hold her, but the weight is starting to hurt my legs."

"Sure, babe." I pressed pause and lifted Austyn from his lap. He let out a long sigh, rubbing the tops of his legs as he looked at us longingly. At her last doctor's appointment, she weighed seventeen pounds. With the fat and muscle padding of Nick's thighs depleted, it must have felt like a whole lot more to him.

"What do you think you will want to do with the video?" I asked.

"I think we should share it," he answered matter-of-factly.

"You do? Like you mean with our family then?" He hadn't been sure when we started filming if he would ever want to show anyone other than Austyn. But part way through recording, he had pivoted saying he might want to show it to more than just her.

"No. I mean, with *everyone* actually. Online. Let's share it with everybody so anybody who might need some hope has a chance to see." His smile was wide and sure.

My blog had picked up more followers every month, and we'd continued getting emails from readers who were impacted by the way

Nick was living out his life. Letters of encouragement poured in too, addressed to Nick, addressed to me, and addressed to our little girl. There were countless messages from people who said #TeamMagnotti was synonymous with hope for them. Nick even got a text from his old buddy Jay who'd decided, after a lifetime of floating around as an agnostic, that he wanted to have a relationship with Jesus too.

"Okay. If that's what you want, that's what we'll do." I smiled back and tried to hide my surprise at the confidence in his answer. "I could message my friend Matt and see if he could edit it so it flows a little better and doesn't have all the breaks or me sniffling in the background."[1]

"Sounds like a plan! Now can you help me get off this couch?" His smile almost reached his eyes, but not quite. He looked so very tired. "I need to go lie down."

I took Austyn into our disheveled bedroom and placed her in her bassinet so I could safely help Nick get up. Instead of the clean lines I was used to, every surface was now crowded with extra IV lines, puke buckets, and hand sanitizer. Even Nick's hospice bed was tucked right up next to our queen-sized mattress.

Hurrying back to him, I shook my head at the me who had worked so many hours just to be able to afford a house like this while missing out on so many hours with my person. Now, I was recording as much footage as I could to remember him.

At Thanksgiving, Nick didn't get out of bed for longer than an hour all day. He didn't eat a single bite of food—no turkey, no mashed

---

1   Nick's video, The Young Father Battling Cancer with a Smile: madefor-brave.com/nick

potatoes, not even a crumb of a dinner roll. I couldn't avoid the reality no matter how hard I tried: I was actually losing my husband.

The hospice nurses began visiting daily. I saw the concern and pity in their eyes as they tried to get Nick comfortable. They set me up with a social worker and asked if I wanted to see a chaplain. I politely declined.

Pastor Eric visited often and assured us he was available whenever we needed him, even at a moment's notice. Pastor Eric and I first really started talking when I was nineteen when he helped walk my family through my parent's divorce. Later, Nick and I would ask him to do our premarital counseling and officiate our wedding.

Similar in age to my dad, they reminded me a bit of each other. At a time in my life when I wouldn't let my dad near me, Eric's friendship was more than welcome. I didn't know at first just how close we would eventually become. Over the years, he turned into a true friend whom I could talk to about just about anything.

But whenever the nurses or anyone I wasn't *incredibly* close to asked me how I was, I'd say, "I'm fine," and smile while bouncing Austyn on my hip to keep her happy. I wasn't really fine. But I knew there wasn't anything anyone could do, so why say otherwise?

Our family was in and out. Nick's dad and my dad often came over to bring groceries and make meals or watch Austyn while I met with nurses and learned how to manage Nick's ever-growing list of medications.

I did my best every day, but I was exhausted. Nick often woke up screaming in pain at night, and Austyn woke up often to nurse. Between the two of them, I was lucky if I got more than ninety minutes of sleep at a time.

One night I had just fallen back to sleep from feeding Austyn when Nick's shouts woke me. I shot out of bed to help.

"I'm here, babe. What do you need?" I said, keeping my voice low.

"I need to go to the bathroom."

"Do you want to use the bedpan the nurse left?"

"No. I don't need *that!*"

I smiled at his stubborn defiance. It was the same defiance he had shown the first time he told me he loved me seven years prior and then when he'd vehemently refused a wheelchair at the hospital just two years before. *Thank God some things never change.*

He struggled to sit up all the way from his barely reclined hospice bed. I leveraged all my body weight to hoist him to a seated position. This was getting easier by the day as he got lighter and my arms got stronger from carrying around our growing baby girl. I lowered his bed and lifted his legs, one at a time, over the edge so his feet could touch the ground.

"Are you good?" I asked.

"Yup. Let's go!"

After he was finished, he requested we stop at the little couch that sat halfway between our bed and the bathroom. I was so focused on keeping him upright I wasn't even sure I'd heard him correctly. He was shakier than he had ever been.

"Stop here, love. I need to pray."

My eyes burned with startled tears. He bent his legs in an attempt to kneel in front of that old couch. Bolstering his back with my shins, hands around his sides, I held him as he bent over the cushions, hands clasped.

"Dear Jesus," he breathed. If I had let go, he would have toppled to the side, so I kept a firm grip. "You have been so good to me. *So good* to me. I am so blessed by the people in my life. I cannot thank You enough for giving me such a wonderful, beautiful wife and little girl. I don't deserve them."

Tears poured from my eyes as I sensed a distinct presence in the room with us. It felt like I'd stepped in on an intimate conversation between two longtime friends. I tried not to move as the warming presence got closer and surrounded us.

"God, I don't understand this. I don't want to leave them. But I know You have a plan, and it's a good one." His voice broke, and he said, "I'm so, so tired of fighting. It really hurts . . . God!" A small cry escaped him.

I bit my lip hard, trying to hold my own cries back as tears streamed down my own cheeks.

"If You're ready for me to come home, I'm ready too. If You need me to stay longer though, I can. Honestly, just Your will, whatever it is. Use my pain, my suffering for Your glory. Just do with me what You know is best. And, please, God, please, just be with Alyssa and Austyn. Take care of them." His voice was heavy with emotion. "I love You, God. Amen."

I couldn't say a word. My eyes burned hot, my throat stung, my heart beat fast against my chest. After just a few minutes, Nick wanted to stand back up. His knees ached and were now bright red from the pressure. The peaceful presence slowly drifted away as my focus shifted, and I helped my husband, who now weighed less than I did, back into bed.

Like so many nights before, I used the buttons to recline his bed first, propped his legs up with pillows, and stuffed more around his arms and along his sides. I laid a blanket over him, tucking in the corners as he liked. By the time I was done, less than a minute had passed, but he had already peacefully fallen back to sleep.

That night I lay awake for hours, tears streaming down my face. *Why Nick? Why? Why? It should be me in that bed.* He was the better parent, the better person with the much stronger faith.

I couldn't believe I was losing Nick . . . and I couldn't believe at twenty-seven years of age he felt *ready.*

I definitely wasn't.

A few days later, Nick's bones ached, and he needed a change from the hospice bed, so I propped him up in a recliner close to the TV in our room. I turned the volume way down and flipped on *Friends*, more for me than for him. He was awake, but I knew he would be sleeping again soon.

"Do you need anything else? I'm going to take a shower," I asked Nick as I situated the baby monitor so I could hear if he needed me. I hated leaving his side and didn't do it often. Instead, Austyn and I spent most of our days doing everything in our bedroom, so we could be nearby.

"Can I talk to you?" Nick asked, his voice noticeably weaker than before.

"Of course, babe." I always spoke softly around him now.

"I know you don't like me talking about this, Alyssa, but I have to say it . . . now."

I knew what he wanted to talk about. He'd been trying for weeks. I took a deep breath and braced myself, nodding at him to continue. I hadn't wanted to listen to any talk of what it would be like when he died because I didn't want to picture it. I didn't want to think negatively. I didn't want to believe it was real. But now I knew I needed to listen. I would bury my discomfort. I would bury my rage over his condition. I would listen. I would do anything he asked.

"You were made for relationship, love. I see it in you every day."

He paused and took a few breaths as I waited in silence, fighting back tears.

"I've told Pastor Eric and a few of our friends, too. Because I want them to remind you. But . . . I want you to find someone to love again. And if he makes you happy and takes care of you, if you know that God is on the same page, then I don't want you to hesitate. I need you to know that I want you to get married again . . . that I hope that you do." He managed a smile, his words clear and sincere.

I knelt by his chair and took his hand in mine, laying my head lightly across his arm, trying to somehow pass on some of my strength. How I wished I could give him my life, give him my health. I could barely speak. "I don't want to find anyone else. I just want you to stay. Please don't leave."

"I want to stay too, love." He sighed. "I just don't know if I'm going to be able to make that happen." He lifted his hand and stroked my hair for the shortest moment. Then he was too tired and laid it down again.

A few minutes passed, and he was asleep. I didn't want to move so stayed by his side, holding his hand until Austyn woke from her nap and tore me away.

Chapter *ELEVEN*

Then I Wondered What Would Happen to Us

THROUGHOUT THE COLD MONTH of December, Nick's cancer spread, and his body continued to weaken. Time felt as if it was passing slowly and quickly all at once. The days were long, and the nights were even longer.

I kept up with my blog as often as I could but struggled to find the motivation to dissect and express my feelings. I didn't have much time, but in between every single *have to* that a young mom faces, I squeezed in minutes of *want to*. And I had only one want—to simply be by Nick's side, our baby girl happily squished between us.

I set up an artificial Christmas tree I'd picked up at Goodwill in the middle of our bedroom where Nick would see it whenever his eyes opened. Our vaulted ceilings allowed me to plop a lit angel right on top of the seven-foot secondhand beauty. I'd never been one for fake trees, but desperate times call for desperate measures. We needed hope now more than ever.

One day a few weeks before Christmas as I was putting Austyn down for a nap, I thought about what lay ahead. I knew I would need to have another hard conversation with my husband. I knew if I didn't get answers to these questions now, I might regret it forever. So I *had* to ask.

"Babe . . ."

"Yes, love?" I sat facing Nick at the foot of his bed where he was propped up, my notebook in my hand. I realized I was clenching my teeth. I forced myself to take a calming breath before I began.

"Where do you want Austyn to go to school?" My voice cracked as I asked my first question.

His eyebrows shot up. "What do you mean? She's a baby!"

Picturing a world without Nick to talk to was paralyzing. I couldn't believe we were having this conversation. It felt surreal—as if I was living someone else's life. My breath caught. I felt as if I was falling, but then caught myself. *Not yet. Be present. He's here now, Alyssa. Be here now.*

"I know. I just mean, if you don't end up being . . . around, I want to know how you would do it. How you would raise her. Do you think she should be homeschooled or go to private or public school?"

"Oh, I see." He laughed a little. "Well, I guess it depends on her. Do whatever makes sense for her and her personality. If you can afford it, a private school where she could learn about God would be awesome!"

This time, *my* eyebrows shot up. I didn't know how he expected me to be able to afford a private school. With the all questions I had, I wasn't sure I'd *want* to put her into a Christian school anyway. Maybe the drugs were getting to him. *I'll have to analyze that later.* I jotted his answer down.

"When should she be allowed to get her ears pierced?

"When should she be allowed to date?

"Should I give her an allowance?

"What kind of sports should I encourage her to play?"

My questions went on and on. I'd stayed up late getting them all down on paper the night before. They were about our finances, our house, and my job, but centered mostly on how to raise our little girl. The questions had been swarming around my head for days as I'd started to accept that—just maybe—this story wasn't going to end the way I wanted it to.

How could I ever make a lifetime of important decisions on my own? I was sure I'd be completely lost without Nick's advice.

"While we are on this topic . . ." Twenty questions later, he smiled tiredly, and I knew he was nearing the end of his energy stores for the day. "I want to be cremated. Unless you really want to bury me. It's just cheaper and makes more sense, takes up less room. I know they probably won't want to use my organs now, but if they do for research or something, then let them." He shrugged his shoulders. The man was still smiling.

"Oh, and I want to die at home. Unless it becomes too much of a burden on you, then you can ship me off somewhere," he said, managing a sideways grin. "Otherwise, I want to be with you here. I'd prefer it. And remember, the ashes, my body, they won't be me. Same with my stuff. Don't hold on to it out of grief. It's just stuff. If you aren't using it, get rid of it. Don't feel weird or guilty giving it away. I'll always be with you. Everywhere around you. In your heart. But I won't be in my stuff. It's just stuff."

He was so matter of fact in his delivery. Not a hint of doubt. Even on death's doorstep, Nick was only thinking of others.

My heartbeat quickened as a familiar thought came to mind, one I hadn't yet brought up—because I was petrified to ask. "Babe, what if I need to talk to you?"

"Oh, love, don't worry. I really think I'll be able to communicate with you." He smiled sincerely and wiped a tear away from my cheek.

"How? And how do you know?" I asked as sobs shook me, threatening their escape.

"I don't know how. But I'm pretty sure." Nick seemed as confident about this as anything else. "There's gotta be a way."

I wasn't sure in the least. *Dear God! What nightmare am I living?*

On New Year's Day, a hospice nurse told me Nick was now actively dying. He hadn't been downstairs since Christmas morning when he'd forced his body to work one last time. He'd opened presents with his little girl in front of her very first Christmas tree. But since that day everything had gone downhill fast. He was no longer responding cognitively. He'd have sudden bursts of energy when he'd haphazardly try to force his weakened body out of bed, then become distressed when he was unable to move. He didn't have any strength left. He often called out to me incoherently. When I came to his side, he could no longer tell me what he wanted.

I whispered, "I love you," to him over and over again that week, hoping and praying for a response. Usually I got none. I stared at him for hours, willing him to look at me as he had before. Willing him to tell me he loved me again.

In early January, he responded one last time.

"I love you . . . Alyssa." He used my name. He was serious. He really meant it.

On the morning of January 7, I woke up at 3:30 a.m. hearing Austyn's cry on the baby monitor. I'd moved her to her own room months before when Nick's sleeping trouble had started waking her through the night.

As soon as I opened my eyes, I became aware that Nick's breathing was more labored than usual. I went to his bedside and placed my hand on his, feeling for warmth.

"You'll know he's close if his hands are cold," the hospice nurse had said.

His hands, which had been characteristically warm, strong, and comforting every single day of our lives together were now weak and frail and *very* cold.

He'll be fine until you get back. I heard the words as if someone had spoken them right to me.

I opened my computer and pressed play on Nick's favorite playlist before leaning over to kiss him on the forehead. "I love you, Nick. Forever and a day. I'll be right back," I whispered. He lay incredibly still. I switched the receiver on the monitor so the sound now came from our room, took the unit with me and made my way to Austyn, who was tossing and turning in her crib just across the loft.

As I sat and rocked our sweet little girl while she nursed, I couldn't help the tears from falling. I knew this was it. This would be her father's last night on this earth. Austyn was barely nine months old. Her pudgy little fingers innocently curled around my hand. Her blue eyes were wide, studying my face as she drank.

"It's going to be okay, little love," I whispered. Tears ran down my face, over my chest, and around her little lips. I leaned my head back against the chair, willing myself to hold it together a little while longer and asking the tears to stop. A short time later, she was peacefully sleeping again. As I laid Austyn back down in her crib, warm and beautiful, I felt a familiar presence wash over me. Like a blanket surrounding me, an ocean of comfort to drown in. The peace reminded me of that night by the couch when Nick prayed. I wasn't alone.

When I got back to our room, Nick's breaths were off. Long pauses stretched between each one.

About a week before, Nick's dad asked if he could be with us when Nick took his final breath. At the time, I had answered, "Probably," feeling completely unqualified to make such a decision, wishing I could ask Nick what he thought and unsure of what lay ahead. But in this moment when Nick's very life hung in the space between this world and the next, I realized whatever was coming was coming, no matter who was there to meet it. So I left our room for a moment and leaned over the railing to wake my husband's father who was asleep on my couch. "I think it's time."

I couldn't stand the distance. Nick was already too far away from me. I lay down next to him, careful not to add any weight to his body, but squeezing in as close as I could. As words of encouragement came to me, I whispered them into his ear. It was as if I was coaching him through his own rebirth as he had so lovingly coached me through the birth of our little girl.

"It's going to be okay, Nick. It's going to be okay. I love you so much. You are so strong. We are going to be okay, baby. Go see Jesus. Tell Him you love Him. I'm so excited for you. You get to go home. You are so loved, Nick. I'm going to miss you so much. I love you. Forever and a day . . ."

At 4:50 a.m. on January 7, 2014, at only 27 years old, my very best friend breathed his final exhale on this earth and his first inhale in the presence of God. It was almost as if Nicholas Magnotti had simply made the decision to step through the gates of Heaven, like he knew that he was going exactly where he was meant to be.

But the second he left, I lost my purpose. I lost my direction. I wanted to go with him, but I couldn't. I didn't know what to do. I lay by his side for only a moment, then I left the room. Then I paced back in again. I wrung my hands. I wandered down the hallways. As people came and said their final farewells, I opened the door for them and tried to smile, but my mouth didn't really work like that anymore.

When I went back into our room to see him one last time, I realized he truly had gone. The body left behind was *not* Nick. I was amazed at how much spirit had occupied his now lifeless form just an hour before.

Sometime later, I found myself on the couch, Austyn was still sleeping, much later than usual. *Grace.* My mom's arms were wrapped around my shoulders as we cried. I watched as two young men carried a narrow black bag down the stairs and through my front door. I should have known what was in that bag. But as hard as I tried, I couldn't understand what they had taken.

"I have to go upstairs," I said suddenly, running up the steps two at a time. My parents followed close behind, trying to understand as I feverishly sprinted down the hall. Entering our bedroom, I saw the empty bed.

Collapsing straight into it, I felt as if a black pit had opened up somewhere inside me. The darkness felt as if it would swallow me whole. It was as if I didn't exist. I no longer felt like a person. I felt like a vacuum sucking everything in around me until nothing at all was left—not the weird smell, not Nick's ring on the nightstand, not the people, not the room. Nothing. Suddenly, I was aware of a guttural sound filling my ears. *Where is that awful noise coming from?* Eventually I realized it was me. It was the sound of deep grief. The pain was profound. Physically blinding. All consuming. I was drowning in the deepest, darkest ocean.

How would I ever break free?

Chapter TWELVE

Then I Tried to Run Away from My Questions

I'D SPENT FIVE YEARS as Nick's wife. Our bond felt as if it had been strongly forged in wartime and reinforced every time we'd scraped through tragedies together. For six years, we'd been best friends, fighting life at each other's side. Us against the world. We'd gone through marital problems, career changes, and health issues. We'd faced broken dreams, a miscarriage, and countless hospital stays. We went through hell together; it's just that Nick never made it back.

I didn't know what to do without him. I didn't know who I was without him. I didn't know how to feel without him.

Immediately after Nick died, the details of daily living fell to my father who offered to move in with me to help with the baby. I was incredibly grateful.

Nick had been spot on with his prediction. I really had needed my dad's support throughout Nick's fight, and we'd mended our relationship in ways I never imagined would be possible again, but I never imagined that Nick's advice might one day also protect my very health. My dad, who has always been an excellent chef, started doing the grocery shopping, cooking the meals for us, and forcing me to eat them. If he hadn't, I'm certain I would have forgotten to eat at all.

Knowing Austyn needed me was my only other motivation to force the nourishment down. Later on, I'd recognize the significance of the timing of Austyn's birth. It wasn't lost on me that her presence in my life kept me sane. She truly was a miracle baby. Not only was she born just after a miscarriage, she was born to a father whose body was plagued by cancer and to parents who weren't even "trying." God's timing was perfect: my little girl practically saved my life.

"Nick!" I found myself screaming his name in desperation from the laundry room one morning in early February when I had folded the last of my husband's clothing. Throwing the entire clean load back onto the floor, I stomped all over it, bawling and screaming in frustration. I couldn't stand to have his chores forever finished. What I would have given to wash his dirty underwear just one more time or find traces of his life again! Things were too clean, too empty without him. I wished for messes from the life he was supposed to be living. I found myself missing the laundry piled high and even the medical devices that had previously taken over our home. I longed for a sink that overflowed with dirty dishes.

I saw the small messes Austyn and I made differently now. Our messes were just collateral—beautiful collateral from lives being lived, the kind of collateral I still longed for with Nick. All the messes were miracles in disguise.

Not only was I missing Nick's messes and especially him, it seemed like *he* was missing everything important too. Austyn took her first steps at ten months old, just a few weeks after he died. My little sister, Kinslee, who had come home from college to be with me, was on one side of the room, and I was on the other. I could barely believe it when Austyn crossed the floor between us. I smiled but my heart broke. *Nick should be here to see this.*

Right around then, I started calling Austyn "Silly Goose." Silly Goose morphed into Goose or Goosey and simply stuck. She was as clumsy as the early walking milestone might indicate but was the cutest little thing, toddling around the house, throwing *everything* she could grab hold of onto the floor and barely keeping her balance. It was adorable (and also slightly scary) seeing such a small baby so fearless on her little feet. I really felt like I needed Nick to help me keep her safe.

I spent weeks reliving our lives together, trying to remember everything about him, trying to remember the way he smelled and the way his voice sounded before he was sick. Over the last years of his fight, much had changed and happened in what felt like such a short amount of time.

In May of 2013, just two months after Austyn was born when Nick's bloodwork indicated there *might* be enough change in his tumor growth, he and his doctors decided to try one more last-ditch effort to save his life. Our specialist agreed to do the same "mother of all surgeries" again.

When the day of surgery came, I nervously paced the same waiting room where I'd had such good news just eighteen months before. This time I held our baby girl—and this time the outcome wouldn't be anywhere near what we hoped.

Almost as soon as they opened Nick's abdomen up, they had to stitch him back up again. There was just too much cancer. A few months after this second attempt at the HIPEC surgery, he told me he wanted to write the next update for our blog. This is what he wrote.

> *Even though I have to fight this nasty disease every day of my life, I never have to go at it alone. I am so blessed in this way. I am the richest person alive. I have the best friends and the best family, and I know they would do anything for me . . .*
>
> *About two weeks before Alyssa and I decided to have this surgery done again, my gut started sticking out really far and started to hurt again. I didn't know it at the time, but what was going on was my body was making this fluid in my abdomen. This fluid was pushing on everything. It was scary. Couldn't eat very much or do very much at all. For some reason, I felt like death was in my near future. I don't know if anyone has ever been there. But it's a very scary feeling, very emotional. I spent a lot of my time thinking about the "what ifs." I really don't like living in this state of mind. It's a very sad place to be.*
>
> *But one day, Alyssa, Austyn, and I were at my brother-in-law and sister-in-law's house, hanging out with them and their two daughters. My little niece Maddie (who is almost three) wanted to go ride her tricycle around the block, so Jordan and I took her outside. We walked down to the end of the street and Jordan said, "OK, time to turn around and head back home." Maddie did not like this idea at all. She wanted to go even farther. But it was time to head in, so Jordan turned her around on the tricycle, and we started to head back home. Maddie spent almost the entire ride back crying. I remember thinking she is missing out on all the*

fun she could be having on the ride back, all because the ride out wasn't as long as she wanted. It helped me relate to life.

Why would we spend even one day being sad that our lives may not last as long as we want them to? Every day I spend thinking about the bad things that could happen is a day that I'm missing out on all the joys I have in my life. In a way, I felt like the past few weeks I had been acting like a little kid. Being sad about something and not enjoying the fun right in front of me. This is something we can apply to everyday life.

Just remember when you're feeling down because your day is not going the way you had planned it that there is still so much in your day to enjoy, and if you focus on that one bad thing you will miss out on all the good.

I did my best to remember Nick's words and focus on the good in front of me instead of complaining about the good that was over. But most of the time, that felt easier said than done.

The hours after Nick passed blurred together and felt like days. And every day felt like a year. By the time nine months had passed, I could have sworn it had been a lifetime since I'd seen Nick's face.

My little sister moved home for the summer and took up the spare room that used to be my office. With my dad's help with Austyn and now my sister's too, I quickly dove back into part-time work, mainly because it offered a distraction from the pain.

Nick's life insurance policy eased the financial pressure I might have felt to get back into the full-time work force. Funny, I hadn't wanted him to apply for coverage in the first place. In fact, I fought adamantly *against* it.

About a year before Nick had any tummy pain, he came home from work one day and said, "Love, I was talking to a friend at work today, and I really think we should get life insurance."

We were in our early twenties. I thought he was cute trying to "adult" and all, but I also thought he was absolutely crazy. I brushed him off and was annoyed when he brought it up again later that night. Pulling up a spreadsheet, he showed me how we could budget to afford a hefty policy every month. He had already spoken with the insurance agents and gotten the quotes. He'd done his research.

I was appalled. "Babe. Seriously! Those guys are crooks! You realize we would basically be just giving our money away, right? We are going to put hundreds, no . . . probably thousands of dollars into these policies for *decades* and not need them until we are great-grandparents!"

"Well, yeah," he said, smiling a bit sheepishly. "But, just in case . . ."

"We might as well throw our money away!" I was confident in my opinion on the subject. "Who in their right mind gets life insurance in their twenties?"

"I'm not sure why. I just think we should. Promise me you'll at least pray about it tonight?" Nick sighed, sounding defeated.

"Fine!" I snapped back. I was frustrated. *What a silly conversation.* But I promised Nick I would ask God, so that night I said a half-hearted prayer about it when I went to bed.

The next morning, I woke up with insurance on my mind. The words tumbled out of my mouth before I had a chance to think about it. "Okay, babe. If *you* think it's a good idea, go ahead and get everything set up for the life insurance." I shook my head as I said it, feeling like a sucker.

In the end, we set up the automatic payments and promptly forgot about the policy that was less than half of what was suggested. To save money (and face), I had refused to go all in. In hindsight, that policy was just more proof that my future was already being taken care of without my even knowing it.

One evening after putting Austyn to bed, I dialed Pastor Eric's number. He picked up my call on the first ring. *Thank God . . . or whomever*, I thought.

"Hey, Pastor Eric! It's Alyssa. Can we talk?"

"Of course, friend. I always have time to talk to you."

All of my friends were fresh out of college at this point, and I didn't want to drag them down with my gloomy mood. I wasn't scheduled to see my grief counselor for another week. But Pastor Eric went to school for stuff like this, and he genuinely seemed to enjoy our conversations. Never one to waste time, I got to the point and let my worries pour out.

"What will I do on the day Austyn gets married?

"Who will walk her down the aisle?

"How will I work *and* take care of her?

"Which school am I going to send her to?

"How will I decide where to live?

"What will I do . . ." My voice trailed off as I started to cry. I couldn't picture my life without Nick. My questions were endless. I had my notebooks full of his recorded answers, but it wasn't the same.

"Oh, Alyssa. I'm so sorry. I can't imagine . . ."

I was glad Pastor Eric never said, "I know what you are going through," even though, of course, he had experienced grief of his own.

He knew because all of our struggles and our relationships are different, nobody can ever truly understand the depth of another person's grief. Whenever people told me they couldn't imagine the way I was feeling, at least I knew they were telling the truth. It was so much better than when people told me they could understand when I knew they most assuredly couldn't. None of us can. Hearing others admit they didn't fully get it made me more comfortable with my grief. I knew there was no right or wrong way to deal with loss. This was all new to me and, as hard as it was to accept, I knew every loss would be new to me for the rest of my life. No two would ever be the same.

Pastor Eric asked, "Do you remember our talk just before Nick started chemo? You were so worried. Do you remember you said you wouldn't be able to get through it? You were worried about the baby. And you had no clue how things would work out financially. But, what happened? Did you starve? Did you lose the house?"

"No." I sighed in agreement. "We were taken care of."

"Right." He paused for a moment, letting it sink in. "And do you remember before Nick died, you told me that you were 100 percent certain you would die too? That you knew you wouldn't be able to go on living without him. Do you remember that?"

"Yeah, and I *have* nearly died," I said, not feeling the least bit overdramatic.

"Nearly. But not quite."

He had a point. I guess my heart was physically still beating even if I wasn't sure I wanted it to.

"Remember this: every time we try to imagine what the future might be like, we are picturing it *without* God's grace or His presence. Since that time hasn't happened yet, our worries are completely false. We are making up in our heads what we think will happen. But we forget that God will be there. And when we get to that time, that scenario in the future, His grace and His presence will cover us."

As soon as Pastor Eric said it, a couple of puzzle pieces came together in an otherwise chaotic mess. Worrying about my future really was so senseless because whatever my brain conjured up would not factor in how much I might grow between now and then. And it wouldn't take into account God's power or presence. At this point, I wasn't quite sure what I believed. But there was a lot I couldn't possibly know in the present, so trying to assume how I might deal with the future was pointless. Worry at its core is always pointless. Why spend time thinking about things that may never happen? I knew it was easier said than done, but this helped.

"Alyssa, this is so hard, and my heart breaks for you." Eric's voice sounded shaky on the other end, and I knew he was trying not to cry. "I miss Nick too . . . so much." The two of them had grown close. He paused and cleared his throat.

"I know God will be with you as Austyn gets older. Every single day, He will walk by your side. If you are open to letting Him, His presence and favor will help you through the days you'd think would be impossible. Your future is brighter than you can see."

I hung up a little later, thankful for our conversation. But I couldn't help thinking, *I hope he is right.*

I was harboring a lot of doubt at the time even though miracles were playing out right then, before my blind eyes. As a lover of soccer, there aren't many other sports teams I followed religiously, but the Seattle Seahawks have always been more than a football team. For many Washingtonians, being a "twelfth man" is a way of life. The Hawks consider their fans to be just as much a part of the team as the eleven who play on the field, and we happily accept that responsibility.

I'd always loved our boys, and Nick had been a longtime fan of the team, sporting his favorite Hawk's gear whenever he could. The Seahawks work their tails off every season but seemed to kick particularly massive booty during Nick's cancer fight, providing hope and wins when Nick needed them most.

When head coach Pete Carroll and the team heard about Nick's love for them and his battle after his cancer returned, they sent him his very own exclusive team gear and autographed ball. Nick lit up like a firework! When they heard about the Seattle Geek Roast, they donated similar items to auction off during the live fundraiser at the event. The crowd went crazy! And in an insanely generous gesture, just a couple of weeks before his last birthday on earth, a few of the players invited Nick to tour their training facilities.

He was beyond excited! When the day of the tour finally came, Nick was too sick to go. But Golden Tate, who played wide receiver for the Hawks at the time, graciously put together an incredible video tour so Nick wouldn't miss out entirely.[2]

At the end of the recording, Tate passed the mic around the locker room. Richard Sherman wished Nick the best. Tate said, "Just know we're praying for you. We are praying for your family. Stay strong, man . . . God has a plan." And quarterback Russell Wilson promised to shoot for the championship in Nick's name, saying, "Hopefully, we can bring home the Super Bowl for you, Nick." The video arrived just days after Nick began hospice care, and the smile it brought to his face was priceless. That was miracle 1.

I'd missed a few of their games that season because I was too busy holding a puke bucket for my husband, a bottle for our baby, or the pieces of my broken heart together. So when I watched them win the NFC Championship after Nick died, I could barely believe my eyes! Our team was going to the Super Bowl!

My dad, a friend of mine, and I shouted and danced in hushed victory from the living room while Austyn napped upstairs. Tears

---

2   To see the video the Hawks made for Nick, visit: madeforbrave.com/seahawks.

squeezed out of the corner of my eyes. I hoped Nick had somehow been able to see.

My phone rang a few mornings after that incredible game. I was still living in what I now call "the fog," that crazy period after big loss where timelines evaporate and every day runs into the next.

"We've got two tickets to the Super Bowl in New York with your name on them, Alyssa. We'll cover airfare and hotel. You just have to show up." Overlake Christian Church in Redmond was offering me the chance of a lifetime.

"Come again?"

When I couldn't quite wrap my head around the words I'd heard on the phone, Pastor Mike Howerton and Pastor Dan Hamer came to my house to personally deliver the news. The church had anonymously received two tickets and was asked to pass them on to someone who needed a smile. The pastoral team had heard of Nick's love of the Hawks, seen the video of the Golden Tate tour, and somehow decided I should be the recipient of the donation. Miracle 2.

At first I was speechless, then I wanted to say no. Survivor's guilt is real. Finally, I realized Nick would have killed me if I turned down an opportunity like that. *Who was I to say no just because I felt sad and scared?* I swallowed my fear and accepted the generous gift.

As we made travel plans, we found all the New York hotels were booked. Right when we were about to give up hope, I got an email from Jackie, a woman I had met through our appendix cancer Facebook group. Jackie offered us the use of her apartment on the upper west side, just steps from Central Park. Miracle 3.

There was no way I was going to be away from Austyn, so it was decided my best friend, Cat, would be my guest at the game. And because they weren't paying for a hotel after all, Overlake offered to fly my dad out with us so he could babysit from the apartment during the main event. Miracle 4.

The trip to New York was incredible, and the night of the game was magical. It felt as if so much more was hanging in the balance than a championship and a trophy. The Seahawks won the Super Bowl, beating the Broncos forty-three to eight, the largest margin of victory for an underdog at the Championship. Miracle 5. It felt like they really had done it for Nick. And it felt like Nick was there, standing by my side through every single minute of it.

Local TV stations picked up on the story of a young woman who got to go to the Super Bowl all because of incredibly generous gifts from strangers. An interview aired with my story featured on Seattle's KOMO 4 before I left and they asked to shoot another interview with the same host, Jon Humbert, while I was in New York which aired the day before the big game. I wasn't too sure about doing the interviews in the first place but I was glad I did when so many people reached out to tell me they were encouraged to hear something so wonderful had come along after my loss.

A couple strangers reached out to tell me quite cruel things as well, even going as far as to call me names for my apparent lack of grief. Because they'd seen me muster up smiles on tv, they seemingly couldn't imagine the sobs that shook my body every night. According to them, going to a football game in Nick's honor, and watching his favorite team bring home the title for the biggest Championship in America was disrespectful. I did my best to focus on the good messages and what I knew in my heart Nick would have wanted.

Days after the game, I opened yet another message on Facebook from someone I had never met. This time I was amazed at what I read. The same day the Hawks locked in their place for the Super Bowl by beating the 49ers in the NFC Championship, the day I had danced in the living room with my dad, Aaron Molksness found out his own father was very ill. A short time later, Aaron's name came up in a lottery drawing for the opportunity to buy tickets to the Super Bowl. Not wanting to miss his chance, he bought the tickets, hoping he might be able to take his dad to the upcoming game.

His message read, "The day I bought the tickets from the Seahawks, my dad died. God led me to give the tickets to Overlake Church as an act of faith, and I did that. I took them to my church and told them to use them for God. I did not know what they did with them until I saw the amazing news story about you and your husband, and I was so deeply moved by your powerful witness. God has a purpose for everything, and I believe this is God's hand directly working in our lives."

If the team hadn't done the video tour for Nick in the first place, the church might not have known. If the story hadn't been in the news, Aaron might not have gotten the chance to see how his gift and obedience was a part of a domino effect that gave one young widow so much hope, in such a dark and confusing time. That trip became a cherished memory I would look back on for years to come as a source of hope and strength. If I could take my baby girl to New York, a city I'd always dreamed of visiting with her dad, then just maybe I was more capable as a mother than I often felt.

"Dad, would you look at my mouth?" I asked, coming into the living room holding the side of my cheek open after having just put Austyn to bed. "How many do you see?"

Dad peered into my mouth, clicking on the flashlight app on his phone. My mystery symptoms had all but vanished during the last year of Nick's life. I found out it was my high levels of adrenaline during that time that kept them away. But as soon as my life started settling into a pace that didn't resemble an ultramarathon runner's, my body began to break down again.

"One, two, umm . . . seven." He grimaced. "I can see *at least* seven. But it looks like maybe more down your throat?"

"That explains why it's been hurting so bad again," I said, tears stinging my eyes. I knew from experience that seven sores meant I was just getting started. I still got thirty to fifty visible sores at a time, not counting the ones that ran down my throat or into my ear canals.

A few days later I was so fatigued from my fever that even sitting upright at the kitchen table was difficult. My fever was low but it was already starting to rise. It would be near 104 degrees within twenty-four hours. Just like in every other episode before, my spine was now throbbing, my back muscles were extremely tight, and my neck was excruciatingly sore.

I spooned pureed zucchini into Austyn's mouth, wishing I could force myself to eat something too. But there was no way to eat past the pain when I was like this. I wiped her mouth while she bantered on with her baby talk, saying "Momma" and smearing her hands through the pile of green mush that had fallen from the spoon.

"Have you ever been tested for something called Behcet's?" my dad asked from the across the room as he looked at his tablet. He'd also been researching my symptoms for years. "It sounds like you. Might be worth checking out."

A few weeks later, I found myself at a rheumatologist's office exploring my dad's hunch. After a battery of questions and blood tests, I had an answer. Eight years of waiting, of doctors' and hospital bills, and wondering what it could possibly be, I finally had a diagnosis.

"You have Behcet's disease. It's an autoimmune disease, a form of vasculitis, an inflammation of the blood vessels. It's technically incurable, but the steroids you have been using are the same ones we recommend to help manage the symptoms. I'm sorry," the doctor said.

"Sorry?" I said, smiling wide. "Doctor, I finally don't feel like a crazy person. I mean it stinks it can't be cured. But I'm glad to finally know what it is!"

I left the office with a newfound appreciation for the miracle that was my dad's presence again in my life and a couple of prescriptions the doc thought were worth a try. I decided as I made my way home that day, I wouldn't take the word "incurable" to heart.

The first thing I did when I got home was dive into research. I would do anything I could to avoid being on steroids for the rest of my life. I scoured the internet for blog posts related to the natural treatment of Behcet's disease. After so much experience researching alternative treatments and medical stuff when Nick was sick, I felt like a pro.

As the leaves began to change color that fall, I still hadn't found a way to avoid my disease entirely. But I *had* discovered a new tool for my fight. Alum, a spice available at most local grocery stores, would painfully burn and then blissfully numb my mouth sores long enough so I could eat, speak, and swallow. Progress!

At least now I didn't feel as weak because I was getting some nutrition. I got so excited I tried skipping my steroids, but the symptoms recurred swiftly. Tail between my legs, I went to my doctor who upped my dosage to get everything back under control.

On the plus side, more steroids meant I was well enough to get my life back in order for the first time since Nick left. Big things started happening—like I was actually getting dressed in real clothes!

It felt good to get out of my sweat pants a few days a week, but I still wasn't feeling great. In fact, I was extra irritable. It was hard to tell for sure if these were side effects of the steroids or because I had some pretty intense things to be upset about. Everything in our small town was *really* starting to bug me. It all just reminded me so much of Nick.

To add to the noisy memories everywhere I went, our house was entirely too big without Nick's laughter to fill it. Unable to sleep, I often roamed the halls at night. The vast spaces relentlessly mocked me and the dreams I'd once clung to. My four bedrooms, formal dining room, eating nook, and bonus room weren't working for me—they were perfect for a *family*. Nick's voice echoed in my head, "We'll have enough kids to fill every room and then some!"

I felt stuck in that town and stuck in that house. I felt if I stayed, I would forever relive the worst parts of my life. I needed to move. Far away.

I tried to tell myself it wasn't just because of the grief or just because of the incredible heaviness in my chest that materialized every time I stepped through the front door. But, really, that might have been most of it.

My grief counselor said, "You have to understand there are a lot of people out there who don't think it's a good idea to make big decisions within a year of a loss like yours." He was wise, and his counsel had proven very helpful to me up to this point. I knew he'd walked many widows, widowers, and families before me through unspeakable grief. I had reasons to trust him.

"That being said," he added. "I don't think moving is necessarily a bad idea for *you* and your situation in particular." He smiled warmly. "I've gotten to know you over this last year, and I don't say this to everyone, but I think you're strong. I think you're good at separating your feelings from your cognitive decision-making. If you think this is the right thing to do, then I fully support you, even if some people end up coming against you." He leaned forward in his chair as he studied my reaction.

I'm not sure if he really thought I had it together or if he'd just seen the stubborn fire in my eyes. Either way, his confidence gave me the push to pull the trigger. I didn't know much anymore, but I knew I *had* to get out of Washington. And there was nothing anybody would be able to do about it.

"I'm taking a sabbatical," I announced to my family over dinner. They reacted with a lot of shock and very little awe. I couldn't blame them. But I wasn't scared. *What could go wrong?* I'd already lived through my worst nightmare.

I decided I would go to Pensacola, Florida and try it out for a month before I made the final decision. That's what solo parents did, right? Well, not the Florida thing so much. The state isn't necessarily chock-full of widowed parents. My thinking was solo parents and widows have to make decisions for their families on their own. They even go on trips on their own. So I thought I might as well start owning up to my new title. I didn't think Florida would be a long-term move, but I needed time and space to heal.

There were a couple of things that put Pensacola on my radar, one main one being the cost of living was much lower than in the Seattle area. I wanted to continue to pursue my writing career, and I figured if my overhead costs were low, I would have a better chance of success. I could still book clients from anywhere in the world because of the virtual nature of my work, so I would be able to keep my prices up. Another reason being that a guy I'd met online kept sending me pictures of Pensacola's beautiful, white-sandy beaches. He loved living there and knew Pensacola popped up on the list of the cheapest beaches to live on in the US. Plus, if I liked the beach well enough and took this little step (well, more like, gigantic leap) across the country, maybe I could finally find some peace.

When I first arrived at the tiny airport in western Florida, the humidity hit me like a ton of bricks. But it felt great! It was a relief to find even the air was different here. Austyn shouted "Alm twees!" over and over when she noticed the towering palms around us. That month away was glorious. It felt a little lonely and sad, but the break from talking to most of the people I knew felt awesome. I had a good excuse to keep to myself—or rather, 3,000 miles of good excuses. It was a true rest, a respite, a calming pause in the nonstop nightmare I'd been living.

Austyn and I slept in every morning. Bright sunlight streamed through the front window of our Airbnb as I sipped my coffee and watched Austyn play with the suitcase of toys I packed. I worked my freelance writing contracts during her naps and made the most of the janky Wi-Fi connection. On the days I was up for it, I slathered us in sunscreen, and we spent hours on the incredibly white beach or splashing in the pool at our condo complex.

I prayed when I awoke but shut my heart up the second I started to really *feel* anything because I was too afraid to face it. I started to go to church on Sundays when my new guy friend invited me, but most of the things the pastor said just seemed to roll in one ear and fly right out the other. At night, I'd bathe Austyn to wash off all the sand and all the sunscreen. Once she was in bed, I watched a lot of Netflix and ate a lot of ice cream. Aside from the day-to-day activity that comes with being a single working mom, I did my best to ignore the hurt I was feeling. It was harder to forget the crushing pain in the dark so I did anything I could think of to numb it until I finally fell asleep.

During my time by the beach, I was very aware I had entered a calm before the storm. I could almost see something big and ominous looming in my not-too-distant future, like a hurricane just off the coast. I tried to pretend as if I didn't feel it but, sure enough, what lay ahead would be one of the darkest parts of my journey yet.

"Hi, Pumpkin!" Dad sounded cheery when I picked up the phone. "How are you doing?"

I didn't go longer than forty-eight hours without hearing from him, via text at least, but I didn't mind. After all, his little girl had jumped a plane with his grandchild and a ticket to the furthest end of the country.

"It's going good, I guess." I sighed, considering what to say next. "It feels good to have some distance from it all, you know? I feel better than I have in a long time, in a way. Freer. And the ocean right outside my window feels good for my *soul*!" I laughed a little as I emphasized the last word with the southern drawl I'd heard around town. We *were* practically across the street from Alabama.

Dad laughed. "Well, good! How's Austyn?"

"She's great!" It was true; she really was. Austyn was still so young she probably didn't even realize we weren't in Washington anymore.

"And before you ask, yes, Dad. We are staying safe. I mean, like I've said before, not *everything* about this place is perfect . . ." I let myself stop there as I didn't need to go over it again.

Actually, everything about this part of Florida was vastly different from my life back home—the food, the stores, the trees. There were a lot of comforting things like southern drawls, jazz bands, and gumbo. But there were also things that worried my dad a little—like gangs, gators, and gale-force winds. Seattle was boring and rainy during the fall whereas the Gulf was all blue skies one day and hurricane warnings the next, always volatile and uncertain, just like my heart.

As our conversation came to a close, I knew I needed to tell him. "Dad, I've decided I'm ready to sell the house." I couldn't imagine ever going back to live permanently in the home Nick and I shared. I was ready. "I'm moving to Florida."

He asked a few questions but, for the most part, took it in stride. That's my dad for you, supportive to a fault.

"Are you going to buy? I know you'll make good money selling the house here." I was honestly taken aback by his question. It hadn't even crossed my mind. Just thinking about making *permanent* life changes for more than a few seconds made my skin crawl. "No, I will not be buying. This will not be permanent." I would move here for a year, maybe two, but that was it.

I think I heard him breathe a sigh of relief.

I wasn't ready to make permanent life decisions, but I was decidedly ready to move on from the home Nick and I had shared so much heartbreak in. Once back home, with the help of one of my besties who also happens to be my bomb real estate agent, I got my house on the market. Within five days, I had an offer for over asking price. I signed on the dotted line as fast as I could. The contract gave me thirty days to get everything moved out.

That's when I realized just how big an undertaking this would be—more like moving mountains than just moving out of a house. Everything Nick and I had ever owned, plus a lifetime of our collected dreams, was scattered and stored and stuffed into our 3,200 square feet of space: the furniture we'd picked out together, the thrift store treasures we'd found, Nick's books, tools, electronics, and spare car parts. If Nick and I hadn't talked about what he wanted me to do with all of his stuff, I might have rented out a warehouse just to store it all.

"Keep nothing in your home that you do not know to be useful or beautiful" became my project motto alongside, "Remember, my stuff is not me." I basically had three sets of criteria to work through. Anything that wasn't useful or beautiful had to go. Then anything that didn't make sense to ship across fifty states had to go. Lastly, anything that wouldn't fit into the one-thousand-square-foot Pensacola townhouse—you guessed it—had to go. I tried to stay focused on what mattered. I would never give up the good memories, but I sold or gave away almost 70 percent of our stuff. I kept three large boxes full of the most meaningful of Nick's things, planning to eventually put them in memory chests for Austyn and myself. His clothes and other personal effects went to his family.

The month passed quickly with so much to do. Once I said all of my goodbyes, I hopped on a plane with Austyn in tow. But just as soon as the plane took off, when there was absolutely no going back, I panicked, *Have I just made a colossal mistake?*

When our stuff, traveling by semi, finally caught up to us a little over a week later, it solidified the reality that I most assuredly had.

Chapter THIRTEEN

Instead I Ran Right into My Answer

MOVE-IN DAY WAS MADNESS. It wasn't until I was putting Austyn to bed that I realized I'd forgotten to wash her sheets, which smelled like the freeway. My pillows had somehow ended up in the same box as the crumb-filled toaster. And to top it all off, I couldn't find the toilet paper.

That night I sank onto my pillowless bed in a room filled with unpacked boxes containing what was left of my life and questioned my sanity, too exhausted to cry. *Why did I move across the country, so far from family? With a toddler? Why did I do this to myself?* I couldn't even leave the house to grab an emergency ration of Ben & Jerry's because Austyn, who had thrown an epic fit before bed, was already asleep on her sheetless mattress. This was going to be harder than I thought.

Eventually I settled in well enough. But despite the near constant eighty-degree weather and a few new friendships, nothing about Florida felt right. Not even close. In that one way, it felt much the same as home.

My business kept rolling along as I continued writing blog posts, social media posts, and web content for my clients in Seattle. I enrolled Austyn in a preschool so I could work for a few uninterrupted hours in the mornings. When I picked up a few local contracts, my income increased. Best of all, those contracts presented me golden opportunities to actually speak with adults!

I even started going to church again, though admittedly, it was mainly on account of the free childcare. Ever since my move, I'd felt a shift in my heart. I was lonely, I was hurting, and I blamed God for it. I didn't give Him the time of day during the week or even much of my attention on Sundays. I was pretty upset with Him, to be honest, and my cold-shoulder treatment seemed like the appropriate response.

When my guy friend officially became my boyfriend, my internal instability and issues with God only seemed to worsen, not all at once, but exponentially as time went on. A little older than I, he was divorced with no kids and served on the worship team at the church I attended. I honestly didn't realize I was in survival mode at the time. I didn't spend too much time thinking about whether or not I wanted another relationship or even whether I was ready to start dating again. *Nothing* felt right from the moment Nick died, so when this cute guy came along with all sorts of confidence and an intense interest in me, I found him hard to ignore and blindly went along for the ride. And adding in a new relationship meant adding in a new distraction from the questions that haunted me.

My surroundings were different in this coastal Florida town with its white, sandy beaches and constant humidity, but I was not as far removed from my problems as I wanted to believe.

The townhouse I rented was a two-story unit minutes from the beach, equipped with a garage, a backyard, and three bedrooms. Despite the square footage, rent was cheap. It should have been a perfect launching pad for a girl trying to start over mostly from scratch. But the days and nights in our new place were some of the longest of my life.

Austyn had always been a good sleeper. Out of desperation, I'd sleep-trained her at five months, and she'd been sleeping mostly through the night since. By eighteen months, she was out for around twelve hours a night *and* napping three hours a day. Lucky me! Right?

Not in this case. In this season, it was painfully isolating. For company, I invited my boyfriend over whenever I could. I also made a *ton* of phone calls—anything to avoid the quiet.

"Hey, Kinslee!" I waved as my sister's face popped up on Skype. My laptop was perched on the kitchen counter that evening, just like so many nights before. My boyfriend was off at band practice, and I was making dinner and dying for some adult conversation. Austyn was playing with empty Tupperware at my feet, but sometimes I just needed more than baby babble with my two-year-old, as wonderful as that was.

"Hey, sister!" Kinslee smiled through the screen from the apartment she was renting with a few girls on her university soccer team in Southern California. "Whatcha doing?"

"Oh, you know, making spaghetti . . . again!" My laugh turned into a grimace. Most nights it was spaghetti or a frozen pizza. My comfort foods had always been Italian. So had my comfort. *Oh, Nick.*

"Want to say hi to Austyn?" I put the wooden spoon I'd been using to stir the jarred sauce down on a plate and held up the laptop so the camera pointed in the right direction.

"Say hi to Auntie Kiki," I cooed.

"Hiiiiii, Keeeekeeee!" Austyn waved her chubby fingers at the screen with a wide gummy grin.

"Oh my goodness, she is so cute!" Kinslee squealed.

"I know, right?" I got the computer situated again so I could get back to the stove. "I miss you, sis . . ."

"I miss you too." I sighed. We were suddenly somber.

"How are you doing, really?" my sister asked. Four years younger, she always had a way of seeing right through me. We'd been pretty close growing up, and the older we got, the closer we became.

"I'm good, for the most part. I mean, it's okay. But I do really think it's good for me to be here, you know?"

"Yeah, I know," she said, reassuringly.

"I mean, I just feel more tucked away, which is nice. My memories were just staring me right in the face every day, no matter what I did. And here, everything is just so . . . different. It kind of feels like I'm giving my heart a break, I guess." I sighed heavily.

"Yeah, I bet. I'm so sorry, sister."

Kinslee always tried to understand as much as she could. Nick had been just like an older brother to her. I wondered if school afforded her the same "luxury" that Florida offered me—an escape from the reality of Nick's absence back home.

When Kinslee asked about church, I quickly shifted the conversation away from my faith. I was having some serious doubts in that department. There'd been a few times I'd asked for God's help halfheartedly, wondering what He thought about my new relationship or asking for healing for Austyn who had developed a nasty cough. But God didn't seem interested. I no longer felt His peaceful presence or heard His voice. I felt completely abandoned, entirely alone.

Because of God's perceived silence, I marched ahead in my new relationship. I figured if I was making the wrong moves, I might as well go big or go home . . . and I *definitely* wasn't going home.

It's not that the guy I was dating was necessarily a bad guy; he wasn't. He was actually really nice—but he was still broken up over his divorce. In the end, I think his brokenness fed into my pain, and then my pain just exacerbated his hurt. Not a great combo. But no matter how wrong it felt, against my better judgment, I kept trying to make it work. Because when he touched me . . . I forgot about all the pain and loneliness, if only for a moment.

I had been a virgin up until the day I married Nick. With him, I knew I was supposed to wait until after our "I dos," and I did. So did he. We'd started our marriage off with our convictions securely intact. It had been hard enough for me to make it to our wedding day, but no one told me what I was supposed to do if my husband died when I was in my twenties.

My boyfriend in Florida had several reasons why he didn't think abstinence made sense between us. I listened, eventually giving in to the most powerful drug I knew. I thought if I satisfied my intense longing to be known . . . it would satisfy my need for love. I thought I would finally feel whole again. I was wrong. Any good feelings I felt in those moments of intimacy vanished almost immediately once it was over.

Sex. Too much wine. Hours and hours of Netflix. They became my crutches. But the castles I built at night to protect myself crumpled around me each morning like sand. I felt emptier than I ever had before, and all my efforts did nothing to fix it. Eventually, I admitted it to myself. I was in a bad spot, and I hated myself for it. But I kept trying to pretend otherwise. I kept trying to pretend I was fine.

Because of all that pretending, I was getting sicker as my autoimmune disease fed off my stress. Being sick made me even more dependent on my boyfriend, which made me even angrier at myself . . . which stressed me out more . . . which made me sicker. I was stuck in a downward spiral and felt as if I was being eaten alive by my bad choices.

One morning I woke up alone and completely fed up with it all. My room was a mess, just like my life. Bathed in clear, bright sunlight, I saw everything for what it was—not just my boyfriend's clothes on the floor, but the deception in my heart.

"I'm so sorry." I wasn't sure who I was apologizing to exactly as I breathed the words aloud, sobbing, head in my hands. But mostly I think I was saying sorry to myself. I still didn't know what my purpose was anymore, but I knew I was made for more than what I'd allowed my life to become.

Sitting in the middle of my bed, through a flood of tears, I made a decision. I would face the places where my soul was weak. I had to stop trying to cover up my questions. I had to stop ignoring the things that were bothering my heart. I didn't know what in the world could help build up again someone who felt as low as I felt, but I was going to do my best to find out.

I knew facing the pain I'd been trying to bury would require gobs of courage. It would ultimately mean stripping away all the temporary fixes and taking a good hard look at the wounds festering in my heart.

The first step had to be breaking up with my boyfriend. It would be hard, although staying in the same situation would have been hard too. I knew it was time to choose my "hard," and I absolutely knew which one I preferred. Facing my demons would be better than living stuck in that vicious cycle. I would rather be alone and lonely than live with the wrong guy for the rest of my life.

"I need space," I told him later that day. That wasn't easy. The moment I said it out loud and saw his face, I wondered if I was wrong. My heart ached, and he was extremely upset, but I knew at the very least, I needed to gain perspective on the situation.

After he left, I called Kinslee. "I did it," I said into the phone as I gazed at the palm tree out the kitchen window. My little sister was about the only one who knew about the doubts I'd held about our relationship.

She breathed a sigh of relief. "Oh, Alyssa. I'm sorry. But I'm so proud of you." I could sense her smile on the other end of the line. "How are you doing?" she asked, sympathetically.

"Good, actually." I was smiling through tears now too. "Being alone here is intimidating, but I know I can figure it out."

After just a few days, I felt even more confident than before. It was clear. I didn't just need space. Our relationship was decidedly over. I wasn't sure exactly what lay ahead, but I knew I would have to go it alone, whatever it was. The almost constant quarantine that followed that decision gave me ample time to think. I started wrestling with myself a little, but mostly with God.

I knew the thing I'd been most avoiding was exactly what needed resolving. I'd been slowly pushing God away for much of my adult life. When it seemed like God had taken Nick—or at the very least, allowed

Nick to be taken—I'd completely turned my back and had run in the opposite direction.

The way I saw it, God let me lose the person *He* led me to marry! I felt betrayed and cheated. I felt lied to. God, who was supposed to love me, had seemingly taken advantage of me. He was supposed to have power over *everything,* but He hadn't done *anything. If* God loved me so much (and that was a big *if),* why did He let all these bad things happen to me?

I finally stopped trying to create a roar in my life louder than my questions. My uncertainties loomed large, finally where they'd been begging to be—front and center. I dove in, feeling as if my life depended on finding answers. In some ways it did because the *way* I lived my life would absolutely depend on what I discovered. If God didn't exist, or if He was just a big meanie, then what was the point of doing *anything* the "right" way?

As soon as I'd gotten rid of most of my unhealthy distractions, I found I had hours to spend on my search. In the mornings, I worked on my contracts while Austyn was in daycare. During the afternoons when she napped and then again after she went to bed, I continued my search from my kitchen counter. My Google search bar could have lit on fire with how feverishly I used it.

Starting at square one with the proposed existence of God, I researched the writings of those who had gone before me on this quest of spiritual discovery. I wanted to know if the One who I was blaming for my pain even existed. Was the big bang theory actually more accurate? Or was there really a higher power out there who allegedly created everything, including torturous cancers that starved beautiful young people all the way to their incredibly slow and painful deaths? (Imagine me shaking my fist here. . . I was one pissed widow.)

I read articles, blog posts, and tore through book after book. I studied and read and highlighted and took notes and studied some more. I watched endless YouTube videos and even read a handful of personal accounts of encounters with God and the afterlife by people from all sorts of belief backgrounds and walks of life.

During this time, I got a better handle than you might think on the single mom thing. Austyn was growing up so fast, and I felt a little guilty for dragging her to Florida. I didn't want to waste any more of my time with her. Always intuitive, she could sense my emotions, so I worked hard during the day to stay out of my head and focus on building an even stronger relationship with her. I made abundantly sure I stayed on top of my meds to avoid getting sick, and I stocked up on household necessities during the day since I knew I would be locked inside my house when she was asleep. I soaked up my time with her as best I could, but my soul practically ached to fast forward to the times when I could go back to working through my existential crisis.

I worked so many hours at my computer that I moved my desk from the guest space that doubled as an office to a corner in my room so my papers were always beside me, even at night. I often awoke in the early morning hours to read and journal and then read some more.

"Momma . . ." A sleepy-eyed Austyn walked into my room one morning dragging her favorite blanket behind her. "What are you doin'?"

"Hey, Goosey! How did you sleep?" I smiled. "I'm just doing some soul study."

"What's dat?" she asked, ever curious.

"Well, Momma is just reading about . . . God, I guess."

"Oh, God? I know Him! He loves us sooo much, Momma!" Her smile was huge as she crawled into my lap.

I giggled at her sweet words and squeezed her tight, planting loud kisses on her cheeks. Oh, how I wished I could still be as confident as she was. I wanted to *know* God loved us beyond a shadow of a doubt. I was searching for a *real* faith. It couldn't be a blind one.

I thought about the times in my life when the universe seemed so obviously slanted in my favor. Those were experiences I just couldn't force myself to believe were accidents. There were all the miracles I'd seen over the course of the last few years. Things that couldn't have been accidents. The airline miles that people gave us to get us to Nick's appointments, the $50,000 raised at the Geek Roast, the free ultrasounds, the life insurance, Austyn herself, and the Super Bowl trip.

Then I thought back further to things that seemed so horrible at the time but had turned out to be good. Like if I hadn't gotten sick and dropped out of college, I would have never met Nick. Or if he hadn't fallen off a ladder at work, he would have never met Robyn at the chiropractor's office who introduced him to me.

If everything had gone according to *my* life plan, I wouldn't have met Nick until I was in my thirties. There's no way we would have had time to get to know each other before he became terminally ill. There's no way our future would have been the same. No way we would have had Austyn, who was my everything.

Then there was that experience I had as a kid. I still remember that night in vivid detail. I was seven years old and Robyn had come over to babysit so my parents could go to a dinner. Just a few minutes after my mom and dad left, I was in the bathroom when I heard a deep, soothing voice speak to me saying, "Pray for your parents." It didn't even startle me, instead I felt completely at peace, though curious. *Where did that voice come from? Why should I pray?* I finished up quickly and ran straight into the other room with my little heart pounding.

I'd looked around and noted the television and radio were both off. There were no sounds other than those of my siblings and Robyn playing. "Did you guys hear that?"

"What?" Robyn asked.

"I just heard somebody, a man's voice, say, 'Pray for your parents.'"

Robyn's eyes got wide for a moment. Then she sat my little sister down on her lap matter-of-factly and held out her hands to my brother and me and said, "Well . . . let's pray for them then!" And that's exactly what we did.

As we got back to our play, I tried to shake off the uneasy feeling that something might be wrong. The next morning, over her cup of coffee and my bowl of cereal, my mom told me she had something to tell me.

"Last night, when your dad and I were on our way to dinner . . ." she began.

"Wait!" I'd interrupted, eyes wide. "Did you and dad almost get into a really bad accident? Because something told me that might happen and we should pray." The look on my mom's face was complete shock.

They'd been traveling down a two-lane highway, just minutes from our house, when a car traveling the opposite way crossed the center line going 60 miles an hour. They, and a handful of other vehicles spun out, slamming their brakes and trying to avoid collision. My mother watched as a large truck came screeching toward them, sideways, headed straight toward her passenger door only to suddenly stop a mere inch away from impact. "It felt like a miracle," my mom said with tears in her eyes as she recounted the scary events that could have been so much worse.

When I thought back to that night, I remembered the words, the voice, the calming presence. *Someone* talked to me. *Someone* knew what was happening miles away.

Then there was the similar presence I'd felt with Nick that night on the couch and again in Austyn's room the night he died. There was clearly more to this life than I could physically see or touch. There was Someone or Something bigger out there.

After some consideration, I had to face the truth: I wasn't going to be able to prove to myself there is no God. In fact, my personal experiences alone proved quite the opposite.

So if God *does* exist then who is He? What is He like? I wasn't quite sure I could even stomach calling him God anymore. The God of my childhood didn't seem to fit. I didn't want to just blindly accept what my parents had taught me or what I'd learned in Sunday school.

I decided I would discount everything I thought I knew and everything I'd learned in my safe little bubble. Things were different now that I'd stared true suffering straight in the face. Losing Nick turned everything I thought I knew about a God who loves and protects us completely on its head.

Determined to find out more about the Big Guy Upstairs and His supposed love, I began repeating a new mantra every morning: "Show me You. Show me truth." And I tried my best to open my heart enough to hear the answer.

Right after Nick died, Nick's YouTube video had come to the attention of a young author named Jefferson Bethke who sent me a signed copy of his book, *Jesus Is Greater Than Religion*. I hadn't read it before because I'd been so focused on trying to prove God didn't exist that I didn't want to muck it up with any "Jesus talk." But I had held onto his book through the move and, once I cracked it open, I found it surprisingly and insanely relevant to my search.

The book was such a gift during this time it might as well have come with a big red bow on top. The God Jefferson knew wasn't the one I had fabricated growing up. His God didn't care what religion you were a part of. He didn't care for religion at all. In fact, He sent Jesus to abolish religion altogether.

I read somewhere that trying to understand God is compared to a gnat attempting to understand humans. But that wasn't going to stop me from trying. I dove into more books, more research, and explored the details behind this truth. What I came to realize rocked my world. Had I misunderstood God in a critical sense? I found all humanity's perception of God was so wrong that He sent Jesus to demonstrate to us a clear picture of who He is. Jesus is a living, breathing, personal example of who God is. He is literally all compassion, all love, and all mercy.

After a bunch more reading and note-taking, I felt like I was getting a handle on a few things. One, Jesus' example was clear. Two, Jesus was all love . . . which should mean God is all love too. But that part still didn't compute with me. If God is all love, why does evil exist? Why do bad things happen? I clearly had some more digging to do.

The thought of going back to the same church as my ex-boyfriend was too awkward for me to handle. But the friendships with the women I'd met there continued to blossom and keep me grounded during my spiritual search.

Genna, a kick-butt mom of three and a transplant to the area like me, became a lifeline. We'd meet up with packed picnic lunches at parks around town to talk about anything and everything as we pushed our kids on the swings. I told her a bit about what I was trying to uncover. It was refreshing to be able to inspect what I was learning out loud and hear her point of view. Genna was from New Jersey so she always shared what she thought (blunt and honest people are my favorite) and provided a judgment-free zone for me to say what I pleased. I valued her opinion

"You've been through so much. How do *you* deal with the whole God-loves-us-but-still-lets-bad-things-happen thing?" I asked one day.

"I've messed up so many times, Alyssa. But despite it all, He has always been there. Always. He is constant. And full of mercy. And love. I feel it. I just know it." My friend was gorgeous on the outside, but her heart overflowed with an unbelievable beauty that I'd only ever seen in those who believed unequivocally in God's grace.

"I still don't understand why Nick had to die," I said to my mom who had offered to clean up my condo's kitchen after breakfast while I finished up some work at the counter. Her visit to Florida at the end of May provided a sweet and brief distraction from the questions my heart had been asking. Mom's faith was solid as a rock, though I saw her beliefs as a tad bit more legalistic that mine, ever since she'd left the Catholic church at nineteen.

"I know, honey, I don't either." Sensing my pain, she moved to my side.

My mom had known an incredible amount of heartache in her own life, but most of the hardships I'd heard about from her as a kid were rooted in her past, before she'd accepted Jesus as the sole reason for her salvation. I think somewhere in my childhood, based on not just my mother's stories but on so many others, I'd subconsciously assumed that knowing you are saved by grace and trusting in God's "hedge of protection" meant you would be safe from the trials of this world. It's like I thought accepting Jesus meant you got a get-out-of-pain-free card when that is never the case.

"I'm so sorry, sweetie." My mom squeezed my shoulders tight. "I'm not sure we will ever understand."

Tears slipped down my cheeks as I realized faith would always be a leap. I still wasn't sure I wanted to jump back in, especially with those who labeled themselves as "Christian." Truth be told, Christians had been the least helpful during the worst of my grief. When Nick was sick, and especially right after he died, people unknowingly offered up some well-meaning but offensive platitudes. The worst one in my opinion was "It's part of God's plan." I got this comment or something like it at least once a week. It was infuriating.

Nick's torturous death was a part of God's plan? What about my grief? Or the future grief of his daughter? What about the even worse suffering that goes on around the world on a daily basis?

I needed to know for myself, so I dug deeper. My studies and prayer led me to a definitive answer. No, the bad stuff is actually *not* a part of God's plan. Not at all. It was *never ever* supposed to be like this. Saying a bad thing is a "part of God's plan" minimizes the pain of those who are grieving. It suggests they might be lacking in the faith department; worst of all, it implies God might actually be to blame, when in fact, He *hates* the evil stuff. He abhors it.

So where *does* evil fit into this whole mess? Does God have less control than we assume? Or does He have a twisted sense of humor? If God has *all* the power in the world, then why does He allow bad things to happen?

The deeper I dove, the more answers started to take shape. Bad things happen and evil exists because without evil, there wouldn't be choice . . . and you need choice to have love. Let me explain.

Imagine if God created a world full of humans who *had* to love Him, who were forced to have a relationship with Him. It wouldn't be a relationship at all, would it? That's more like slavery. And God didn't want a world of robot-slaves. He wanted to create people he could have a relationship with. He wanted to create love. Love by its very nature has to be a choice. There had to be light *and* darkness, good *and* evil, choosing Him or choosing *something else.*

Cause and effect are a natural part of having created human beings who can choose Him or choose the "other." The domino effect of so many poor decisions has brought this world to where we are today. But none of the bad is *because* of God.

When bad things happen as a result of the evil in the world, God's heart overflows with sadness right alongside ours. He sobs with us. And, though He *could* stop any of it at any moment, He sees the big picture and knows something about eternity that we don't. Namely, everything!

This new understanding gave me some sure footing in my journey. Breathing finally started to feel a little less like drowning.

To give myself a break from my heavy research, I planned outings nearly every day. Austyn and I shopped, visited coffee shops, beaches, farmer's markets, and flower stands. The quiet hours after her bedtime, which started at 7 p.m., no longer bothered me. I was on a mission to find truth, and nothing else mattered. The more I uncovered little clues, the closer I felt myself coming to the truth.

Sitting down at my desk one night, I read the story of Job in the Bible and looked up the stories of Ruth and Esther. Then I read of contemporaries who found good coming out of their bad. This mysterious idea that God could use even the bad stuff to create good intrigued me.

Somehow, someway, could God create good out of my mess too? I'd felt hopeful, but the more I thought about it, the more I felt this "good" could never happen for me. I hung my head in despair and whispered a quiet prayer, "I might be losing my mind, but God, I *dare* you to make good of *this.*"

I went to bed feeling hopeless. My hurt ran too deep. My mess was too great. I could feel myself resisting the possibility of good, even still, even after all I'd read. I just didn't believe it could be for me.

The weeks following that God-dare brought brand new misery. Where my grief before felt like waves, the worst of it slowly ebbing and flowing in and out, it now felt like a nonstop tsunami crashing onto shore. The breakers wouldn't stop. Before, so much of my grieving had been full of anger. Grieving for Nick had also been grieving what I thought I deserved from this life and over losing a "god" I'd made up in my head. But after my discoveries, my loss wasn't buried in confusion and rage anymore, instead, it was pure, unadulterated sorrow over losing the love of my life.

One night in the middle of April 2015, about fifteen months after Nick died, I found myself heaving and screaming and slamming my fists into the carpet. I thought I was going to go blind from the pain that consumed me. I got up. I sat down. I paced. At one point, I found myself in the bathroom pressing my body into the corner of the room against the cabinet, wanting so badly to disappear into the wood grain. Aching for an escape, I pressed my fingers against my eyes, screaming in anguish. Not anger. Not denial. But a sharp realization that Nick was never coming back.

Suddenly, another thought hit me out of nowhere. *Somehow, someday . . . I would be okay without him.* As a familiar peace washed over me, I began to sob.

"Jesus, I need You," I cried out. I sensed God was on my side, and He truly loved me. I didn't understand it all, and I probably never would. Though I couldn't believe I was saying it, I told God, "I trust You." I surrendered everything in that moment. I gave Jesus my very life. I didn't have all the answers. I was an absolute wreck. But that night I handed God all of my rubble, all the broken pieces of my life, and took my dare back. Instead of daring Him to create good out of the worst thing that had ever happened to me, I *believed* He would. And I committed to partnering with Him to make it happen.

In that little townhouse in Florida, I found healing. It wasn't like everything changed in an instant, but a big part of me had. I found a deeper relationship with the One who made me, and it transformed me from the inside out. It was like a switch had flipped. I knew without a doubt that God had moved mountains to bring me closer to Him. For what I believe was the first time in my adult life, I truly knew the Creator of the universe had my back. As I lay on my bedroom floor, the words I'd read in the book of Esther echoed through my heart. I was made for such a time as this. I was made to live a life of faith. And a life of faith would always *require* courage. I was *made for brave*.

After picking Austyn up from school one afternoon a couple of weeks later, I drove us out to my favorite beach. Clouds rolled and rumbled in the distance but the sunshine was brilliant on shore. Austyn played on the blanket, ate her fruit snacks, and skipped off to dig in the sand, and I watched the waves lap at the sand.

As I looked out onto the horizon, I could only see the edge of this vast ocean. I realized how much more of it existed beyond what I could see. The perception from shore vs. what was actually out there was worlds apart, but it was the same ocean, the same water.

I think God is a little like that. There are parts of Him we have to brave the storm to see. I found myself thanking God in that moment, not just for the dry land I inhabited now, but for the darkest depths I'd faced. I couldn't believe what I was experiencing. Nick *wasn't* crazy for saying the pain was worth it. It *wasn't* the meds. All of the horrible things I'd faced—the hurt, the pain, the grief—all of it was worth this feeling. *All of it* was worth being closer to the One who created me.

As the storm clouds rolled further out into the distance, Austyn called to me from where she was digging. "Wove you, Momma." She smiled and waved at me, her blue eyes sparkling.

"I love you too, Goosey, forever and ever." I smiled at her even as bittersweet tears stung the corners of my eyes. Looking to the sky, I knew Nick saw us too. "Forever and a day," I whispered. A warm breeze brushed across my face, almost as in response. My heart was at peace. I had all the comfort I needed. I would trust in the Creator of the vastness I hadn't yet seen.

My lease on the Florida townhouse was nearing its end, and I knew it was time to go home. This time when I packed up to move across the country, it didn't feel like a hurried escape. I was technically going backward, but it felt a lot like moving forward. I was stronger. I was braver. And I was definitely better than I'd been before. I felt invincible with God firmly planted in my corner. I felt like I could do anything . . . even move back to where the reality of Nick's absence would never be far from my mind.

Chapter FOURTEEN

Now I Know
Purpose Doesn't Come
Preassembled

WHEN THE PLANE TOUCHED down in Seattle, I felt a deep sense of joy for the first time in a long time. Austyn was cozied up sleeping soundly in the seat beside me. I reached over and caressed her cheek, feeling her soft skin against mine.

"We're going to be okay," I said quietly almost more to myself than to her. It reminded me of all of the times I had whispered those same words to her on the nights our family of three had slept in hospitals across the country. This time, though, I believed it more than I ever had before. I couldn't wipe the smile off my face.

Mom picked us up from the airport, eager to hear about our flight. "How does it feel to be back?" she asked as I shut the passenger door behind me.

"Light," I said, the only word I could think of.

"Light?" she questioned. I turned around in my seat to peek at Austyn who was all smiles, happy to see her "Nama," as all the grandkids call her. I tried again, "It feels good. Sort of weird, but mainly just really good."

Mom reached over and squeezed my arm, "I'm so glad you guys are back, sweetie."

"I am too, Mom," I said with a relieved sigh. And I meant it.

I still missed Nick. I still craved his companionship, his friendship, his love, his smile. And oh how I longed to hear his laugh. But I knew he was okay. I didn't know what the new normal would look like for Austyn and me. I didn't know where we would live or what I would do to make ends meet in this incredibly expensive part of the country, but I had an inner assurance, a crazy peace. Everything was going to work out just fine.

After I got home, I touched base with Pastor Eric, letting him know I'd made it back to the Pacific Northwest. He knew I still had questions, but he had been undeniably happy when he heard what God had revealed to me, or rather what I had finally accepted, in Florida. Talking with him, I had wondered aloud whether a career change would be in my near future. Instead of writing to help other people achieve their goals, I wanted to write more about what I'd discovered in my journey back to hope, but I didn't have the time.

"Have you ever thought of becoming a life coach?" Pastor Eric had asked.

"Who? Me?" I was pretty taken aback at the suggestion. I hardly considered myself one to show others how to live their lives, considering my daughter and I were currently homeless. "No. Why?"

"I don't know, I just have this feeling. I think it's something you should look into. I feel like you are supposed to be helping people find the kind of peace and shift that you've found in your life." He listed off a few more reasons why he thought I would be good at it. "Just think about it."

"Sure." I had shrugged it off as we continued our conversation but later that month found myself thinking about it more and more. I wanted to feel more fulfilled by my work. I remembered what I had told my high school counselor. It was still true. At my core, I just wanted to help people. I was grateful to be writing and working my own hours so I had nothing to complain about, but I began praying consistently for clear purpose in my work. I wanted to write about things that mattered to me for work, not just for my blog. I wanted to do something that helped people. But I still needed to pay the bills. It was a tall order, but if anyone could find a way for me to pursue my passion and keep the lights on, I knew the One who created the universe surely could.

Back in Seattle, for the first time since Nick passed, I felt like I could dream again. Before, I hadn't been able to think ahead or picture a day without Nick. But now things were different. No matter what I did, I knew I would be whole. I would be loved. God would always have my back. Having that assurance was everything.

When I considered my future, I no longer saw endless darkness. Instead I saw a bright blank canvas and an invitation to create my own life. I didn't know where I wanted to live or exactly what kind of life I wanted to create for Austyn and myself, but I knew I wanted it to be a beautiful one.

"Where do you think you want to live?" my friend Cat asked me early one morning. We were nursing our cups of carefully poured artisanal coffee while curled up on her couch. Our longtime best friends had offered to take us in upon our return to the Seattle area. I was humbled at the offer and immediately accepted. I'd always loved hanging out with their family; their new baby girl and her husband, Sean's, love for fancy coffee was icing on the cake.

"I don't know, but for some reason, Seattle just keeps calling my name." I'd never lived within the city limits before, always at least twenty minutes from downtown. But right now, the city sounded perfect.

For weeks I searched, and that search eventually began feeling bleak when I didn't find anything. When I finally stumbled upon a preschool I loved in the Green Lake neighborhood of north Seattle known for its family-friendly atmosphere, it finally narrowed down the options. At least I now had a neighborhood to aim for. But there was one problem: Green Lake wasn't particularly cheap. To add to the cost, a lot of the houses in the area were old and charming, which could also translate to cold and drafty. My budget could only accommodate low heating bills. I needed something I could keep warm and something that felt safe with room enough for a busy toddler. If I really let my daydreams soar, walking distance to the lake would be nice too.

My hopes and wish list were admittedly high, but God kept bringing my heart right back to that neighborhood, so I kept on looking. And I kept on praying.

I scrolled online listings for hours and toured various properties with absolutely no luck. And then it happened. A notification for a new house on the market popped up in my inbox *just* as I was logging onto my computer one morning. My heart skipped a beat as I clicked on the link and practically spit out my coffee in surprise.

The pictures of the new listing were beautiful. A newly refinished house with granite countertops, hardwood floors, three bedrooms, one bath, and a fireplace! It even had a garage and its own fenced yard where I imagined Austyn playing in the summer. Best of all, it was a short, four-block walk to the lake. Even through the computer screen it felt like this house was a direct answer to prayer. *This is supposed to be our home.* I couldn't help but say it out loud. "Wow! It's gorgeous!"

I went with my gut and paid $100 to submit my application, sight unseen. I also attached a letter to my submission to explain what had gone on in my life that resulted in my erratic cross-country moving patterns.

In response to my application, I got a generic invite to an open house. Giddy with excitement, I accepted, and my mom offered to watch Austyn. When I arrived at the address the next weekend, I found twenty other people already waiting outside. A fully remodeled house at a decent price so close to the lake—I should have known.

As I walked through the rooms, the wood floors lovingly creaking beneath me, the house already felt like mine. But that didn't make sense. Other people clearly seemed to love it just as much as I did. They were surely picturing their furniture in each room just like I was. And these were *whole* families: moms *and* dads. *Ugh.*

Less than an hour later, I dragged myself away from the house with a slump in my step. There was no way I would get it. Why would they pick me? In the letter I'd sent along with my application, at risk of sounding like a crazy person, I'd told "Whom It May Concern" just how this property had answered my prayers. But realistically, how far could something like that get me? What did I expect? A pity apartment?

After putting Austyn to bed that night, I was on my laptop and deep in the real estate ads, trying to scout out a more realistic option, when my phone rang.

"Alyssa, this is Becca, the listing agent of the home on 80th." I recognized the voice of the realtor who had opened the house the day before.

"Oh yes! Hi Becca!" I held my breath.

"You got it, girl! The house is yours! The owner read your letter this evening when he was going through applications and decided you're the one. He didn't even want to look at any more. You're *in*!"

After I hung up the phone, I cried in relief, thanking God again and again. Clearly He was watching out for us! I would work my butt off to make the best life possible for my daughter, starting with a house I could make into a home. This was a real shot at our brand new beginning. And I was really ready for it.

Almost immediately after finding out about the house, I got an email from an entrepreneurial newsletter to which I subscribed. The expert urged us to raise our rates, not because of need, but because of the value of our work. It was scary to think of asking for more money, but I knew my rates as they stood were *very* reasonable. Also, I was about to pay first and last month's rent on a house in the most expensive part of the country. So I read a few blog posts on how to convey your professional worth, studied the best way to approach the situation, swallowed my fear, and went for it. I'd started out on the low end of the industry standard when I first launched. But after years of experience, I had more to offer. My writing flowed and had personality. I gave a voice to the brands that trusted me, and I was never late on a project. Plus, I had a little girl who deserved the example of a mom who wasn't afraid to stand up for herself.

Those scary but empowering conversations with my clients led to the dissolution of one contract job. But over the next three weeks I took on two *new* contracts and successfully updated my old rates with the others who were happy to oblige. The new setup paid almost twice as much as before—all because I followed the call to be brave and was crazy enough to believe it just might work.

I was fully comfortable in our new-to-us house almost immediately. It just felt right. I still experienced moments of sadness, but the deep pain in my gut, the feelings of separation and heartache were gone, replaced by a sense of ease.

We settled into our new routine after just a few weeks. I'd even unpacked almost every box. After all, what else was there to do after Austyn was asleep other than to crank Taylor Swift and dance party my way through to organization?

Not everything was rainbows and roses though. Physically speaking, I was a hot mess. I caught every cold under the sun, and Behcet's, my autoimmune disease, continued to stalk me like a jealous boyfriend. Along with being endlessly fatigued, I could barely think when it came to work. I felt like my brain was in a constant muddle.

Life might have dealt me a few ridiculously painful blows, but I was becoming increasingly aware that everything in the universe was under God's direction, and He was on my side. I had survived in Florida, and I knew I could do more than survive here. I could choose to *thrive*, even in my illness . . . even, I could barely believe it, without Nick.

A new dream started to take shape. Now that I knew where I was planting my roots, I began picturing *who* I wanted to be. God would come first in my life, no matter what. Next, I would take care of myself, figure out my health, find a way to be more passionate about my job, and I would take care of my girl. I'd do whatever it took.

In the mornings, Austyn attended the dream Montessori preschool. After dropping her off, I often sprinted down to the coffee shop on the lake and ordered a, "White chocolate Americano with a splash of almond milk, thank you very much." Balancing my coffee and my trusty old MacBook, I'd claim a table or a spot at the busy espresso bar, pop in my earbuds, and get to work. There was a lot to do and not a lot of time to do it, but I always got it done. One to two times a week on our way home from school, Austyn and I would stop by the grocery store to eat lunch in their little café, get groceries, and run other errands on the way home. It felt busy, but it was a relatively simple existence. I mostly loved every minute of it.

I was just near enough to my friends and family that I got to see them on a regular basis. My sister (who now lived just one neighborhood over) and my other Seattle friends occasionally dropped by with a bottle of wine to chat. I'd often walk the trail around Green Lake with my dad or meet up with friends and acquaintances who wanted to kick around a soccer ball or picnic at the park. It was great catching up with everyone again. Austyn loved all the attention and everything felt warm and bright, even after the sun went down and I got back on my computer to work.

When Nick and I first started dating, I'd come across a quote that stuck with me: "Love is when home goes from being a place to being a person." When he got sick, the truth of this was even more apparent. It didn't matter where we were or what hospital we were in, I always felt at home when I was with him.

But now I was without him, and for the very first time in my life, I felt "at home" in my heart. I was safe, and I didn't have to depend on another person or even on four walls to keep me that way. It was true freedom! Nobody could take away my joy.

Despite the crazy pace of single mom life, I intentionally took steps to get even closer to my Maker. I tried to make time every day to read, dive deeper into my studies, while journaling and blogging through the process.

I had changed. I could feel it. Because of what I'd gone through, I was softer, and God was using that to shape me. As I watched for proof of God's love, I chose to deeply love the person God was molding me to be all because of extra helpings of His grace. As much as I was changed and now purposeful with my life, I was still 100 percent human without a doubt.

In my daily prayer time, I'd often pray something like this: "Creator, be with me today. Show me what You want me to do. Lead me to have the conversations You want me to have. Help me to help those You want me to help. Let me see those You want me to see. Amen."

Feeling emotionally stable, I didn't worry about a lot of the things people my age seemed to worry about—careers, men, or school. I didn't wonder constantly what my life would look like in the future or dwell too much on what had happened in the past. I was getting really good at living in the moment. And I loved it. Sure I was tired, and my days were long, with work in the mornings, and more work after bedtime, and corralling a toddler at all times. Single mom life was still harder than anything I had ever done before. But my standard mode of operation was joy. I smiled—a lot.

It was a strange feeling to be stronger mentally and spiritually but so weak physically. On bad days when I battled my Behcet's, I felt as if I was barely able to keep my head above water. I had to choose to hand my health over to God daily and trust Him with it. Some days, just getting out of bed felt like an act of war. It was hard, and I wasn't perfect at it. I constantly begged God for relief. I prayed hard as if my healing fully depended on Him. But I also worked as if the outcome was solely up to me. I tried a few things in the hopes I could feel as good on the outside as I felt on the inside.

My first attempt was joining a gym with childcare where I attempted to make it to class at least three times a week, which proved to be a lot harder than I thought it would be. How anyone can parent, work, and consistently make it to the gym is beyond me. The hour-long workouts and drive time took two hours and more often closer to three. Those were *stressful* times, carting around a cranky toddler when I was already so exhausted from my day. But I tried.

I attempted to eat better too, going back to what I'd learned when Nick was sick. I thought my cure might be in organic foods, less gluten, more veggies, more water, and hundreds of dollars of supplements. These changes felt impossible for a busy single mom, but hey, at least I was doing what I could.

Along with doing everything I could to kick my disease to the curb, there were still a few other things left on my to-do list. For one, I needed to find a new career path—but that task felt insurmountable. Where would I find a job as good as what I had? I was writing from home and could control my workload by deciding how many projects I took a week. I was living every writer's dream, right? *I should just leave it alone.* But something always felt like it was missing.

Then there was the matter of finding a new church home. I knew getting plugged into a community of believers was vital despite my newly acquired distaste for things that smacked of "organized religion," but I wasn't sure where to start.

"So, any new guys I should hear about? Or horrible first dates I can laugh at?" My friend Judy and I met up at the gym that morning. We were sucking down smoothies from the gym's juice bar. I'd chosen the one with the word "energy" in it, game for any excuse to curb the deep tiredness that seemed to have taken up permanent residence in my bones.

"Ha!" I took a sip of my green drink, trying not to grimace. "Nope! I've sworn off guys. Plus, I'm too tired." I knew if anyone would understand, Judy would.

She had stumbled across my blog over a year earlier and had quickly become a good friend. Judy was part of the same club to which I now also belonged—the club nobody really wants to be in—the "young widows club."

At the prompting of my social worker, I had tried to join widows' support groups before. But all of the women in those groups had been at least three decades older than I, some five or six. Judy was a saving grace, an angel my age, someone who had walked the path I was on but who was just few steps ahead.

Her husband and college sweetheart, Keith, had fallen from a parking garage when she was newly pregnant with their son. He had immediately gone into a coma. Keith stayed in that vegetative state through Judy's entire pregnancy and beyond before Judy and his family were forced to make the heartbreaking decision to take him off life support and let him go.

Years later, she was now remarried, their son almost seven, and she had recently given birth to twin girls. I could see redemption in her eyes, I could feel the peace she had found in God and the joy she was experiencing daily from her new love. Her story broke my heart into a million pieces all over again, but it also gave me hope that maybe I could have a family again someday too.

"Is it because of your disease thing?" she asked, compassion etched across her face.

"Yes. Always. But I think it's just this solo-parent life thing too," I said with a sigh. "I can't find the time to get to the gym, or eat right, or find even a church. It's just exhausting trying to get through my days."

"I hear you. I feel the same, and I'm not even sick or single. Life is busy and exhausting in general." Judy smiled and added, "As far as church goes, you can always come with us to ours!"

It sounded like as good a place to start as any so I took her up on her offer the very next weekend. I was determined to do *something* to keep moving forward. When I woke up that Sunday feeling oh-so-tired and wanting nothing more than to go back to sleep, I forced myself to get out of bed. Though Judy's church wouldn't turn out to be an exact match, that Sunday *did* spark an idea.

Of course, I could have mustered up enough courage to go to church by myself if I had to, but I knew a ton of people in the Seattle area. I could tap them for suggestions and tag along each weekend! Not only would it be a great excuse to see my friends, I'd get to scout out churches that had at least been approved by people I knew. I figured that way I'd have a better chance of finding one I liked.

Right away I began reaching out to a handful of folks, asking questions about their places of worship. Half a dozen had churches that sounded right up my alley, and I began marking dates on the calendar to coincide with their attendance. I refused to allow myself to be stressed about being out of my comfort zone every single weekend. Determined to see the silver lining, I told myself this would be an adventure.

"So what do you think, Goosey?" I called across our galley kitchen as I washed dishes at the sink. Austyn was in the family room, stacking her books in huge piles and knocking them over, shrieking with joy every time they fell. Outside it was gloomy, the rain coming down hard. But none of that bothered me anymore. My outlook had changed. My whole life felt so different than it had even just five months earlier. Everything was brighter, more colorful, and more wonderful, even on gray Seattle days.

I focused on the heavenly scent of the vanilla candle that sat lit in the kitchen window as I stacked clean coffee mugs in the cabinet. Our heat was on, and our bills were paid. Rain wasn't anything to complain about. The darkness outside didn't sneak into my heart anymore. I was so grateful for where I was, despite the unknown. I was my own source of light, radiating the love of the One who called me His.

"What, Mom?" Austyn was putting more and more words together these days and it was making me darn proud. My baby girl was growing up, and it was amazing (and frightening) to see how quickly it was happening.

"Mommy has a little bit of work to finish up. After I'm done, do you want to go to Target with me and get snacks?"

"Yesssss!" she squealed, knowing we would share a bag of popcorn as we wandered the aisles. Raising an energetic and stubborn toddler by myself meant I'd figured out a few things we could do together without too much argument from her. Her smile was out of this world. She looked just like her dad. My heart swelled with a familiar sense of bittersweet joy.

Once I'd finished up in the kitchen, I grabbed my laptop and plopped down on the couch to get a little work done. My browser opened to my Facebook feed. Right at the top was a picture of what looked like a church service. The caption read: "Five years ago, I accepted Christ into my life for the first time. Best decision I ever made. At this morning's service led by John Maxwell, hundreds came forward to do the same. God wants you to be a part of His story."

The name above the post made my heart skip a beat. "Jay Galios"— Nick's old club-days' friend. A vivid memory rushed forward of Nick calling out to me across the house years ago, joyously shouting out his news with happy tears in his eyes.

"It's Jay!" he'd said as he smiled wider than I'd ever seen. "He's decided to follow Jesus!"

I'd smiled back. How could I not? I was happy for Nick but completely dumbfounded. Inside I had been thinking, *We'll see how long that lasts.*

Snapping back to the present, I clicked on Jay's profile just to see what kind of life he'd actually been living lately. I'd stayed in touch with most of Nick's old buds by text messages here and there and would see them at mutual friends' get-togethers. I had been close to virtually *all* of Nick's friends. All of them anyway . . . except for Jay.

When his profile finally loaded, I couldn't believe what I saw. Not only was Jay holding down what looked to be an impressive corporate job, he was regularly posting motivational quotes and resources to help other people. According to his bio, he still lived in the Seattle area. On a whim, I sent Jay a quick message to ask if he knew anything about good churches in the area because it seemed from his post he absolutely would.

Hey Jay! Hope you are doing well! I've been trying out a few new (to me) churches in the area, trying to find a new church home. I tried The City Church in Kirkland and saw you are living out there. Have you ever been? Where do you go these days? Hope you are doing well.

I closed the Facebook tab with a little bit of laugh and a reluctant sigh, ready to get to work. It would be pretty ironic if Jay was some sort of link to Austyn and me finding the right church. I was more than ready to settle in with a faith community, no matter who introduced us. I knew the Creator would have me stumbling upon the right location eventually. But I was crossing my fingers it would happen sooner rather than later.

Chapter

FIFTEEN

Now I Know My Creator Always Has My Back

JAY RESPONDED TO MY message later that day. Our conversation centered around local churches and eventually shifted to my new favorite topic: God and the crazy ways He works. Eventually we decided to catch up in person. What I assumed would be *maybe* an hour-long catch up with Nick's old friend and a pleasant little church chat turned into an entire afternoon by the lake.

We'd settled on meeting at a little café not far from my place on a Sunday afternoon. It felt good to see Jay again. "How long has it been?" I asked. "It feels like it's been since our wedding!"

"Actually, it was at Nick's . . . service," he said gently.

"Oh, right." I awkwardly tried to cover my tracks. Along with many of the details of Nick's celebration of life, a list of all those who attended seemed to be forever locked away in some hidden compartment of my brain.

"It's totally fine if you don't remember." Jay smiled empathetically. "You kind of had your hands full." He nodded at Austyn, who was busy running figure eights around us and all of the tables. I often found myself wishing I could borrow some of her unbridled energy.

I ordered one big berry smoothie for Austyn and myself, and Jay got one for himself. We sat down at a little table in the courtyard just outside.

"Tanks, Mom," Austyn said with the biggest purple-smoothie-stained grin after I gave her the first sip of our drink.

I caught Jay watching her smile, shaking his head in awe.

"She looks so much like Nick. I can't believe she's talking now!"

"Right? She does a lot more than just talk now. She's two and a half!" I laughed, retrieving a tiny soccer ball I'd packed in my bag. Austyn snatched the ball from me and threw it to the ground. As she chased it, a few other little kids there joined her, wanting in on the fun. She was always making friends, no matter where we went. People were drawn to her just like everyone had been drawn to her dad. I couldn't help but smile as I watched her play. How blessed I was to be her momma.

As Jay and I talked, I realized I was getting to know him for the first time. When I told him of my love for books, he immediately recommended a few motivational ones and offered to pass on copies of his favorites when we were done.

"Just remind me before you leave! I've got them in my car."

"Wait. You keep them in your car? The books?" I said, surprised. "What do you mean?"

"I grab a bunch of copies from thrift stores and keep them in my trunk, just in case I run into someone that needs one." He shrugged his shoulders as if stocking a free library of inspiration for others in the trunk of his car was normal. I laughed.

The more we spoke, the more I saw just how compassionate he was and genuinely sincere. Corny or not, he was determined to impact the world positively in a big way. I was inspired when I pressed for more information, and he told me he didn't just stock books in his car, his involvement stretched to include serving at his church and participating in international missions.

He'd clearly given up the club life years ago and credited God for his positive lifestyle change. He now worked as an account executive for one of the largest apparel manufacturers and distributors in the world, selling blank apparel to some of the largest brands on the planet. "I love my job," he'd said with a smile. "It's a great job with a great company. I know it's not what I want to do forever, but it definitely works for now. Plus, I get a lot of free clothes!"

"Free clothes?" I asked. He went on to explain he bought extra clothes in bulk on discount through work and brought them to local homeless shelters. I was intrigued. But he only offered more of the details when I wouldn't stop asking. He was confident, but he was exceedingly humble. I didn't remember him having those qualities before.

Jay worked his job from home too, just like me. We found ourselves gushing over the parts of work-from-home life that we loved and laughing about the parts that sometimes proved to be a little more challenging—like forgetting to get dressed until after 3 p.m.

While Austyn played, running back often to tell me what she and her new friends were doing (as if I wasn't watching from just ten feet away), I gave Jay a quick overview of my life. There was just as much he didn't know about me as I didn't know about him.

"Day, do you want to play?" Austyn tugged on Jay's sleeve a while later, trying her best to make the "J" sound but failing adorably.

"Sure!" He laughed and got up to join her.

I noticed his height as he stood. Jay was a runner. Tall, lean, and toned, about six feet tall—he looked so much bigger than Austyn as he sportingly tried to kick the tiny ball with his big feet.

When he finally sat back down, collapsing into the chair and chuckling at Austyn's protest, he admitted he actually hadn't spent much time with kids. He'd grown up an only child and didn't have many family members his age back then or friends with kids now. But for a guy without much experience, he certainly acted like a natural.

A sudden realization hit me: *Jay and I could easily be friends.* I finally understood why Nick had gone to bat for Jay so many times in the past. There really was something special about him.

After we'd slurped down the last of our smoothies, Austyn started to get antsy as two-year-olds sometimes do. I knew she needed to burn off the sugar rush and had planned to walk with her to a nearby park after we were done. Then Austyn took it upon herself to invite "Day" to join us.

"Thank you, Austyn, I'd love to." His smile reached all the way up to his striking bright blue eyes, making them crinkle at the corner.

As I pushed Austyn's stroller toward the nearby park, I said, "You know, when Nick and I first started dating, I used to tell him not to be your friend." I grimaced and then laughed awkwardly. *Oops! That was probably not the nicest thing to say.* Mentally kicking myself, I immediately wished I could take back my words. I'd always been too honest for my own good. I hoped I hadn't hurt his feelings. Trying to backpedal, I added, "I just mean . . . you kind of seemed like a bad influence back then." I stopped when I realized I was just making it worse.

"No, no, it's okay," Jay said. He laughed, his eyes dancing. "I certainly wasn't the *best* influence."

He didn't say it proudly, just matter-of-factly—as if he was stating he had brown hair or lots of freckles. He wasn't hiding that he spent half a decade as a professional partier.

"My life is so much different now. It took me a while to figure out what it meant to follow God after I was saved, but I get it now. Those party days are long behind me."

He was laughing, and I didn't detect a hint of guilt, which felt right to me. I couldn't imagine where I would be without the grace that covered *all* of my mistakes.

When we arrived at the play area, Jay held the stroller in place while I lifted a very excited Austyn out of it. She bolted straight for her usual favorite. Taking turns pushing her on the swings, Austyn giggled as she tried to make us switch places quicker than we could manage. "Now, Mom's turn! Now, Day! Mom! Day! Mom! Day!"

By the end of the whole thing, I was out of breath, and I'd laughed so hard my stomach hurt. I couldn't believe I was hanging out at a kids' playground with a guy whom I'd written off as bad friendship material for my husband almost a decade before.

It was so crazy to think of all the ways I'd doubted God's love for so long before Nick even got sick. I definitely wasn't perfect at trusting His mysterious ways now, but I was getting much better. Whenever I began to doubt these days, I called to mind all the ways God had already worked in my life. How He used my running away to Florida to break me down and build me back up stronger. He'd even used the lines I crossed with my ex-boyfriend in the bedroom to firm up my resolve to stay abstinent now. And, best of all, how He'd used something so horribly bad—losing Nick—to bring me something *so* good—a real relationship with Him. I finally was trusting God's overarching view over my miniscule close-up. Letting go and letting Him lead like that felt incredible.

Jay, Austyn, and I ended up hanging out a few more times in the following weeks, grabbing coffee or going on walks around the lake. I found myself looking forward to his company and his calm, confident presence. As he started to learn Austyn's language, she'd started looking forward to time with him too, often saying "More 'nacks, Day, pwease," because he always obliged.

A few weeks later, I was posted up on the couch, beat after another typical day of work and toddler rearing. Austyn finally in bed, I flicked on a rerun episode of *Friends* and opened my laptop so I could publish my latest blog post and check my inboxes. Between the two blogs I now ran for myself and the consistent social media content I posted, I often got messages from people expressing their sympathy and sharing their own journeys of loss. My posts had definitely taken a happier turn after Florida, which had brought even more hope to many. But my happiness also upset some people who seemed to be angry to see me finding joy and faith again.

That night when I clicked on my inbox, my eyes skipped over the messages from strangers, and a new message from Jay jumped out at me. My heart skipped a beat as I opened it.

I feel kind of awkward asking this, and I know it would be best to discuss in person, but we don't really have plans to connect live for another ten days, and I wanted to see if we're on the same page. Before we met the other week, this had honestly never even crossed my mind, and I want to keep my intentions pure. I know we're just being friendly, but I feel like I am getting the vibe that you may potentially be interested beyond friendship.

My mouth gaped open. I paused my show and read on.

I feel like I know you but not all that well, but based off what I do know and our communication, I know you have many qualities and characteristics that I personally look for in a woman.

Hmm . . . *interesting.* He has a checklist. I was *just* starting to get used to the idea of him being my friend after his sketchy history. I hadn't honestly thought about us being anything more. I was perfectly fine being widowed . . . and single. I'd found my groove. But I did really like hanging out with Jay as a friend.

However, questions arise in my mind. Is this moral? What would Nick think? What would our mutual friends think? Maybe my thinking is flawed, and I care too much what others think and want to maintain a positive reputation. Or maybe it could totally be on the positive side of the spectrum. Or maybe I'm just jumping to conclusions. I don't know what the future holds, but in the meantime I want to build a friendship with you and make sure we sustain boundaries. I'm wondering if, maybe, you feel the same?

I thought back to all the times we'd hung out over the last couple of weeks. I definitely didn't think I'd given off the vibe that I was interested in anything more than a friendship. I *had* noticed recently just how adorable he was. And I was smiling a lot, but that was just me these days. I was happy. I was content. There were quite a few guys who had been asking me out on dates recently probably because I grinned incessantly, and they took that to mean I was flirting. I guess I couldn't blame Jay for thinking we might have something more too.

As I thought more about it though, I realized Jay seemed *different* from all the other guys. Nobody else asked me what Nick would think. Nobody else had Jay's generous heart. And absolutely nobody else had those eyes.

A few months before, I'd written an entry in my journal when I was feeling decidedly over the whole dating scene. The energy it took didn't feel worth it, especially with my disease. So I'd decided I wouldn't say yes to another date unless a list of certain criteria were met. Any guy who so much as wanted to buy me a coffee had to measure up—and I set my bar high. I flipped back through my journal until I came to the entry.

1. *He has to love people. A drive to serve others.*
2. *Needs to have a real relationship with our Creator. Tuned in. On a journey. Probably not a cookie-cutter Christian, but loves Jesus with his whole heart.*
3. *Required: consistent and reliable. He's gotta be someone I can count on.*
4. *Strong values. Incredible level of integrity.*
5. *Courageous. I'm just not attracted to nervous dudes.*
6. *He has to be hot. Natural chemistry is a must. No apologies! He must be confident.*
7. *He has to be someone I can see myself partnering with in all of life.*
8. *Has to be a hard worker. Doesn't give up when things get tough.*
9. *We gotta have fun together. Extra points if he's spontaneous and romantic.*
10. *He has to have a healthy respect for Nick and for what I've been through and love even the bruised parts of me. He has to respect my history.*

As I began going down the list, I checked each item off one by one. Suddenly my heart was fluttering, but I didn't want to get ahead of myself. I sighed and leaned back into the couch. *Jay, huh?* I said a prayer, asking God for direction. And there it was, almost immediately: that distinct, undeniable, indescribable peace.

Swallowing my fear and without overthinking it too much, I agreed to meet up with Jay the next day. But I was definitely *not* going to get my hopes up. I would be just fine if it didn't work out. Besides . . . there was no way I was going to let anything get in the way of the only relationship that really mattered to me now.

I was afraid our first time hanging out since our conversation might feel incredibly awkward like all the other first dates in my life, aside from one. What if it was immediately apparent that I didn't want to be more than friends? What would I say? What if I wasn't attracted to him that way?

As it turned out, I didn't have to worry about any of that. If I had been comfortable before, it felt downright cozy now. If we had talked easily before, we spoke even more effortlessly now. Where I'd noticed his blue eyes before, I was positively drowning in them now. Our surprising new friendship quickly and organically, almost accidentally, grew into something more. It wasn't long before I realized . . . I *liked* him. As much as I absolutely loved the crazy life I was already living, Jay somehow seemed to fit right into it.

Jay was big on God, big on relationships, big on health, and big on reading books to improve his life. He encouraged me to continue to become a better version of myself in ways I'd never been encouraged before. Our early dates consisted of a lot of grocery shopping trips, cooking adventures with my toddler, and long nights staying up late to read side-by-side, just like your favorite geriatric couple. But it was just what my soul needed.

Aside from the fact that things were getting off to what I considered to be a great start, it didn't help that some intense feelings of guilt hit pretty early on.

After a few hours of kid-free fun on a double date with Judy and her second husband, Patrick, Jay, Austyn, and I finally arrived back at my place. Jay offered to carry my sleepy daughter down the hall and tuck her in with bedtime prayers. I happily conceded and used the extra time to change out of my jeans into a pair of sweats and make my way into the kitchen. Tossing a bag of popcorn into the microwave, I ran my hands through my tangled hair as I waited for it to pop.

It felt weird knowing I liked someone this much again—and it felt weird that I trusted someone enough to put my daughter to bed. I heard the two of them giggle in the other room.

I was living such a different story than I could have ever pictured for myself or my little girl. I hadn't expected to find a serious relationship again, *especially* so soon. Not in a million years would I have expected anything to happen with Jay, of all people. But I was feeling good about where we were. It felt natural and right with no tug on my heart to do anything different. Strangely, it felt as if it was exactly where I was supposed to be.

"Well, I better get going. Work day tomorrow." Jay stood up as the credits rolled on a silly rom-com we'd mostly talked through as we munched our popcorn.

"Yeah, it's late, and you have to be up early." He managed East Coast accounts, so his workday often kicked off before the sun was up. I smiled and got up from the couch too, fluffing the pillows back into their proper shape.

"Well, I'll see you tomorrow then?" Jay asked as we walked to the front door. He opened it and turned back for a hug.

I put my arms around his waist as his long arms enveloped me completely. His six feet felt really tall compared to my 5'3" stature. I felt infinitely safe in his embrace.

"Holy cow! Look at those stars!" Pulling away, Jay stepped out onto my front porch, eyes to the sky, and motioned for me to follow. He was always looking up, often taking pictures of the sky, obsessed with the many ways God seemed to paint it.

"Wow! They actually *do* look really bright tonight." I said, pulling my sweater tighter around me. The night was chilly probably because the cloud cover was gone.

"It's 11:11," Jay had glanced at his phone a moment before, noting the time. "Make a wish."

"I don't know what I would wish for. I'm pretty happy right now." I smiled, my back against the frame of the front door that I'd left cracked open behind me.

Jay confidently took a step in my direction, his blue eyes sparkling. "I know what I would wish for . . ." he said, his face inches from mine.

I suddenly became intensely aware of how much I wanted to reach out and touch him.

"Is it too early for me to ask if I can kiss you?" he asked.

A warmth rushed through me, and I realized I didn't just want to touch him. More than anything, I wanted to kiss him. "No, it's not too early." I smiled up at him as he placed one hand on my lower back and the other through my hair and behind my neck.

Ever so slowly, ever so sweetly, he brought his mouth closer to mine. My knees went weak, and my heart raced. When his lips landed on mine, I didn't just feel fireworks, my whole heart felt like it exploded.

I'm not sure how long our first kiss lasted, but it didn't feel long enough. When Jay left, I slipped dizzily back inside, shutting the front door behind me and leaned against it. *Did that really just happen?!*

Over the next few weeks, Jay and I found a way to hang out almost every day. The more we hung out, the more it felt like we'd been together forever. We shared more kisses and even went on a couple more official dates, sans toddler.

One night after one such outing, he cracked a question that I somehow hadn't been expecting, "Alyssa, will you be my girlfriend?"

Everything inside me felt like it came to a screeching halt. *Wait, What?* I wasn't seeing anyone else and didn't have any plans to and neither did he. We were dating. We were *clearly* into each other. But something about putting a label on it freaked me out. Was I really going to be one of Nick's old friends' girlfriends? That was just too weird. Gossip inducing situation aside, was I really ready to commit to an *actual* relationship when I had been so happy and fulfilled without one?

"Jay, I need . . . more convincing." Even as I said it, I knew it was a cover-up to buy myself more time. "I know I would be good for you," I said. "But I don't know the reasons why you would be a good fit for me." Stepping into boyfriend-girlfriend territory with Jay could put me on a slippery slope to falling hard for him. I needed to know how into this he really was.

"I'm up for the challenge," Jay said. He smiled playfully as if my rejection hadn't fazed him. I sighed with relief, glad he was up for it. I honestly wasn't trying to play games. But I still felt I had things I needed to work through before the next step.

The end of our evening felt a bit awkward after my not-quite-encouraging response to his laying his heart on the line. I knew I would need to make a decision soon. Was I really going to go for it with Jay? Or would I choose to tap out on account of fear? I wasn't sure.

About a week later, Jay asked if he could take Austyn and me out to dinner. When he arrived at my house to pick us up, I was still finishing up one last bit of work on a client's blog post. After a quick hug, I sat back down at the computer, trying to focus as Jay pulled a chair up next to mine. I could feel his body inches from me. I typed with force, willing my brain and my fingers to work together to finish.

"Done!" I said as I finally submitted the project.

"Before we go, I need to ask you something." Jay smiled, pulled my chair around to face him, and reached for my hand.

A million butterflies created chaos in my stomach.

"I want to read something to you," he said as he cleared his throat and pulled a folded piece of paper from his pocket. "It's Ten Reasons Why I Will Be Great for Alyssa."

My heart skipped a beat as he started to read. He didn't know I had exactly ten bullet points on my list too.

1. *I will put God as the central focal point of our relationship. Christ will be my guide, my example, my walk. I'm all in as an ambassador for Christ.*
2. *I will be loyal, honest, transparent, and faithfully committed to you.*
3. *I will love Austyn as my own. I will raise her with you, and I will be the best dad I can be.*
4. *I will continuously read, counsel, and seek wisdom to strengthen our relationship.*
5. *I will love you unconditionally through the highs and lows.*
6. *I will uplift, encourage, and support you in your desires.*
7. *I will be there for you in moments of sorrow, and I will pray with you.*
8. *We will keep fun a top priority and do things together that bring us joy.*
9. *I will make your love languages, physical touch and quality time, significant and constantly fill your love tank.*
10. *I will trust my life with you and consistently serve you. I will be your best friend.*

"Wait! Let me see that!" I swiped the paper out of his hand playfully and read over his carefully handwritten note. He was absolutely adorable and undeniably romantic.

"All of that to say, if you'll let me prove it, I *will* be great for you," Jay said. "So I have to ask again . . . I would like to make this official. Alyssa, will you be my girlfriend?"

I'd prayed all week for guidance and the peace I felt in my heart confirmed it was right. It was time to push my fears of the unknown aside and take the leap. I hopped into Jay's lap as happy tears threatened to spill over. "Yes, I'll be your girlfriend!" I put both my hands on either side of his face as his soft lips met mine.

"Thanks for asking . . . again."

Chapter SIXTEEN

Now I Know the Best Is Yet to Come

I SAT IN MY grief counselor's office for the first time in a long time, knowing this latest development called for emergency measures. "How do I choose?" I asked, sounding almost as exasperated as I felt.

It hadn't taken me long to realize my relationship with Jay wasn't going to be a dead end. If I stuck with it, we would go places. Amazing places. But as sure as I was that we were a perfect match, I could still feel myself resisting. The push and pull on my heart was unmistakable. I'd lose control and find freedom in the fall for him. Then I'd suddenly find myself fighting to regain my composure, putting up walls, and throwing negative vibes to protect myself. I couldn't put a name to all of the feelings, but I knew one particularly well—guilt.

When I started thinking about and planning for a future with Jay, part of me felt mortified. When I tried to imagine my new beginning, one where I may be one day married to this incredible human and creating a world-changing impact with him, I felt a block.

How could I build a future without Nick in it? How could I possibly love someone else? And how could I ever marry another man?

I knew Nick hadn't disappeared when his soul left his body. Because I knew he hadn't evaporated into thin air, I wasn't sure how I could move forward. It had been made abundantly clear to me that he was still very much alive, even if I couldn't see him anymore.

About a week after he passed, I'd experienced something that drove this point home. Nick physically visited me. I know it sounds crazy—I do. There's probably no way in the world I could believe it was possible if it hadn't happened to me.

One moment I was in the car alone, on the verge of an emotional breakdown. And then, in the next moment, he was there, riding along in the passenger seat beside me. It was Nick, reassuring me saying, *Everything will be all right, love. God's got you.* I felt his presence so distinctly although I couldn't physically see anyone.

Astonished, I'd pulled the car over to the side of the road and reached my hand into the passenger seat, almost certain I would feel him. Once I'd somewhat recovered, I put the car back in drive, wondering if I was going off the deep end. I prayed as I pulled onto the road, "Umm . . . God? That couldn't have been Nick, *right*? I mean, that's not a thing You do, is it?" I hadn't even finished my thought when a song came roaring through my speakers.

On the last summer we had together, Nick was in the middle of chemo with barely a thread of hope left for a cure. He'd come home from work one day telling me about a song he'd heard that nearly knocked him off his feet. He read the lyrics out loud to me and with tears in both our eyes, he'd declared it "our song."

We didn't dance at our wedding (partly because Nick told me he was embarrassed to dance and mainly because I didn't want people asking why I skipped the father-daughter number). Nick had promised me one day he would find a song we could share. It had taken years, but if there was ever a song that described our lives, then this was it.

"Hey Pretty Girl" is a country song by Kip Moore about two kids who fall in love, build a life together, and grow old. At the end of the song, when the husband's life is clearly hanging in the balance, he thanks the Lord for "a real good life, a pretty little girl, and a beautiful wife." The song bore a striking resemblance to our own love story, down to the color of our little girl's eyes.

That day in the car I didn't remember turning the radio on. But when the song and those end lines played loudly over my car stereo that day, I knew without a doubt that somehow Nick had found his way to "speak" to me.

Tears streamed down my cheeks as I drove west toward the sunset with a smile on my lips and peace in my heart. Nick was okay. He was grateful. One day I knew just maybe I could be both of those things too.

Here I was years after that encounter in the car, more okay than ever before and incredibly grateful. But that's exactly what seemed to be freaking me out.

"What do you mean, 'How do I choose?'"

My grief counselor, a PhD with a penchant for helping me sort through my more complicated thoughts, used his hands to put air quotes around my question, startling me back to the present moment.

I had already spilled all the details about Jay with a ridiculously large smile on my face. Surely this question would stump him as much as it was stumping me.

"I mean . . . how do I choose: Nick or Jay?" Jay was an absolutely incredible guy—a perfect match for who I was today, which was a far cry from the person I'd been when I'd first met Nick. But Nick was an amazing guy too, one with whom I had a deep and complex history—and who was the father of my little girl.

"Alyssa." The doctor looked me straight in the eye, making sure he had my attention. "You. Don't. Have. A. Choice."

"What?" I asked, sincerely surprised.

"You don't have a choice." He paused, clasped his hands in front of him, and leaned forward in his chair while keeping his eyes steadily locked on mine. "Nick is gone. He's not coming back. You can't be with him."

It felt as if I'd had the wind knocked out of me. I tried to maintain my composure, but my body was reacting like I'd just taken a sucker punch to the gut. I took a few gulping breaths, wrung my hands, and started to sweat as I tried to calm my racing heart.

The counselor looked sympathetic but seemed almost as surprised as I felt by my visceral reaction.

"True." I managed one shaky word and tried to walk myself through what was actually happening. *Have I really not processed this? Have I not accepted the facts?* I realized in that moment that I had on multiple occasions subconsciously conjured up alternate realities where Nick had found his way back to me. I'd actually imagined what it would be like to have him come waltzing back into my life. I'd pictured us running into each other decades from now in some far-off country and laughing about the mix-up over his death. I'd recently even found myself wondering what I would do if he were to suddenly return to Seattle and find me married to another man.

I'd chosen Nick every day of my life for almost seven years, and I had planned on choosing him every day for the rest of my life. But the counselor was right. I no longer had that choice.

I'd physically held Nick in my arms as he'd passed from this life to the next. There were no "what ifs" or "somedays." He was indisputably gone. This side of heaven, I wouldn't see him again. A tear slipped down my cheek as this new realization started to take shape.

My counselor leaned across the coffee table to hand me a box of tissues.

"You're right," I said, sniffling. "For some reason . . . in my head, I kept feeling I needed to figure out who I would love more or which one I would choose." I took a deep breath. "I'm realizing now that I'm letting a question trip me up that doesn't even exist."

"Exactly." The counselor smiled sympathetically.

"So what do you think about heaven then?" I asked, knowing this side of life wasn't my only concern. "Have you read the book *Heaven*, by Randy Alcorn?"

The book had just about changed everything I thought I knew about the after-life. When I was still living on the Gulf Coast, I'd read a number of near-death experience accounts about heaven. One book that I kept going back to was *Heaven*. It was the same book Nick had asked me to read aloud from almost every night during his five months of hospice care.

The book answers the question, "What will heaven be like?" from a biblical standpoint. The picture Alcorn paints is truly a beautiful one that had me longing for such a place.

Years of misconception and tradition have given us a skewed perception of the idyllic place that was quite literally created specifically for us. Far from a glorified church service full of boring angels and perfect puffy clouds, it will be all the things on earth that bring us joy: relationships, color, creativity, art, food, beautiful views, teamwork, architecture, love, possibility, breathtaking sunsets, education, and laughter. All completely without blemish.

Imagine the world as it is now completely devoid of the negative influences of death, shame, deceit, disease, cheating, jealousy, lying, dread, comparison, murder, hurt, selfishness, or decay. Currently, darkness and sin touch nearly every part of our existence, even the parts that seem absolutely pure are always in some way tainted.

A world without any of those shadows or hurts would be a place where each and every person is fully loved, fully cherished, fully known, and living that truth out with every single cell in their being. Bad stuff won't exist, and we will still be able to create, love, and live, all without hindrance.

Ever since my newfound relationship with my Creator, I'd actually become excited to end up in that incredible place someday with my Maker physically always by my side. That peaceful presence I'd experienced was something I could only imagine living in continually. The thought took my breath away.

"I have. It's right here, actually." The counselor crossed the room and pulled a tattered copy of the thick book from his floor-to-ceiling bookshelf. "And you know what? This book and the actual Bible is pretty clear that we won't be married in heaven, *per se.*" He smiled.

"Right. But I know we will still have relationships. I know I will remember Nick and everything we shared. And I will remember everything with Jay too. What if *we* have kids together? What if *we* end up together longer than Nick and I ever were? What will I do? Who will I choose then?"

"Personally, I don't think this is a question worth asking right now. I don't really get how it all works, but I don't think you will need to choose between them. I think God will have that part all figured out for us. If for some reason you do have a choice at that time, I think you can trust God to lead in that situation too. You already trust Him so much now. Don't you think He would be capable of helping you choose the right partner for eternity?" He rubbed his chin and smiled as he sat back down. "Remember, like Nick always said, 'God's got it.' Right?"

I flashed back to all the times Nick used to say "God's got it." That saying sure applied here and so did "Let's cross that bridge when we get there."

I agreed, realizing in that moment I needed to surrender the intricacies of not just my relationships in this life but my relationships forever to Him. I would have to let go of my pursuit of another easy black-and-white answer. I had to accept, in faith, that God would work it all out for *eternal* good. My heavenly future, though clearer than ever for me, would always be at least one part mystery until I made it there.

I left the session that day feeling much better. Still, I kept my distance from Jay as I worked through this new bit of awareness. I couldn't see him too much until I was sure I was ready to go all in. Every time we hung out, my soul seemed to take quantum leaps toward his. I don't know if it was destiny or just the natural trajectory of a relationship when a kiddo is involved, but baby steps at this point were entirely out of the question. And, if I was being honest with myself, I was still a little scared.

When I found a seat at my usual coffee shop later that week to get some blog work done, I found my mind hadn't really followed me there. I stared at my blinking cursor for almost an hour before I finally gave up hope of actually being productive. Despite the talk with my counselor, I couldn't get the question "Jay or Nick?" out of my mind. It was driving me crazy!

I picked up my laptop and tossed my half-finished Americano in the trash. I clearly needed some fresh air. After stashing my things in my car, I headed for the trail that went around the lake. Feeling weighed down by the enormity of my emotions, I looked around on the grass for a place to sit. Finding a spot in the shade in this very public place during the middle of a blistering hot summer was always a challenge. Finding a place where I wouldn't be sitting directly in someone's old gum or a steaming pile of dog poo was almost impossible.

When I *finally* found a spot I was certain was void of trash or excrement, I sat down and popped my headphones in so no one would bother me. As I pulled my knees to my chest, my heart ached, my eyes burned, and my head hurt. I didn't want to let Nick "go" in the way I knew I needed to in order to move forward with Jay. After going back and forth for a few minutes, I stubbornly decided I didn't *want* to make room in my heart. It was too scary. I knew I was *made for brave*, but this felt like opening myself up to liability. Loving again would mean being vulnerable to even more pain. It was too risky.

Jay could die just as easily as Nick had.

I'm not putting myself through that again!

My negative thoughts ran wild. There was no way I could do it. Who was I to think I'd be able to find amazing love *twice*? I was crazy to think I had a second chance at being happy after all I'd been through.

I needed to call Jay and tell him I couldn't do it. I had planned on rocking the single mom thing before he came into my life anyway. It would be easier. I could hold onto Nick and my grief and my walls forever that way.

As I leaned back to lie down on the grass, hot tears ran into my ears. I hate when that happens. But right then, I didn't care enough to move. I was exhausted. My heart felt so heavy. I closed my eyes and breathed in and out, trying to focus on calming myself down. I tried not to think about what I would say to break it off with Jay because that just made me cry harder.

"God's got this," I said out loud. "God's got this. It's going to be okay." With every exhale, I tried to let the problem go. I quieted my thoughts and tried to center back on the truth. *I am loved by my Maker. No matter what I choose.*

Maybe it was minutes or maybe it was an hour later, I found myself being startled awake. I had fallen asleep but something had woken me up. I could feel someone nearby watching me. Lifting my head, I looked around. Nobody was there. In fact, compared to the busy summer day I had witnessed just moments before, the lake seemed eerily quiet. I couldn't even hear any noise coming from the usually very busy street behind me.

"Hello?" I called out. The presence was so strong. Sitting all the way up, I twisted around for another look. I peered at a shady spot behind a tree nearby until my eyes adjusted to the brightness, but no one was there either.

Calm flooded over me as I suddenly felt a warmth on my back, which was now facing away from the sun. It was as if someone was sitting behind me, holding me up.

"Nick?" I was suddenly very aware that it was him. My voice caught in my throat as I leaned back and felt my weight supported, my legs out in front of me, my back reclined. *How in the world?*

"Oh, Nick!" Tears ran down my cheeks in torrents as I relaxed into him. He was back! For a split second, I wondered if I was dreaming. But no, I felt so clear. I was here. I was moving my hands, feeling the solid ground beneath me, and breathing in the smell of freshly mown grass. I shook my head in disbelief.

My words came tumbling out in a garbled whisper, "I don't know what to do, babe. I don't want to leave Jay, but I don't want to forget you. I don't know who to choose. I love you so, so much. I won't ever not love you. And I miss you . . . so much. So much . . ." My voice trailed off as I began to sob.

Love, you don't have to choose. The words came clearly to me, as if someone had whispered them right into my ear. *It's okay to fall for him, love. Everything is going to be okay.* I could almost sense him smiling. My tears stopped short in disbelief. I'd heard him so clearly.

I sat straight back up and crossed my legs in front of me to support my own weight again. The warmth immediately left my back, but I refused to turn around again. *There's no way.* I shook my head in an attempt to clear the crazy and wiped my eyes. That could *not* have been real. That last time in the car *had* to have been a fluke, a onetime exception. There was no way this was him over a year and a half later. *No way, no how.*

I ran my fingers under my eyes and then through my hair, willing myself to stop crying like an absolute lunatic at the park. I popped my earbuds out. A couple walked by on the trail laughing happily as they held hands, and their children raced their bikes on the path ahead. I sighed and let my hands fall on the grass in front of me.

That's when I saw it. Right between the place where my hands had fallen, dead center in front of me, was a bottle cap. It was black with one number printed in a white collegiate font *just like* on a baseball jersey. The number was 10. Nick's number. It wasn't buried in the dirt or tucked under blades of grass. Not even one green blade overlapped it. It was literally floating on the tips of the grass as if it had been carefully balanced there for my eyes only. It definitely hadn't been there before.

Later, when I tried to convince myself someone must have slipped something into my coffee, I would reach for the cap in my pocket and run my fingers over it again and again. It had Nick's number, but it might as well have said, "Nick was here."

Chapter SEVENTEEN

Now I Know What You Focus On Expands

AFTER THAT DAY AT the lake with the bottle cap, I jumped in with both feet.

Jay was wonderful. He was everything I could have wanted in a boyfriend at that time in my life and more. He bought me flowers, planned date nights, was great with Austyn, and told me I was beautiful. And best of all, he made me better, bringing me closer to the person I was created to be.

Jay and I were sitting on my front porch steps on a sunny Saturday after lunch, Austyn laughing and running back and forth between us in the yard, picking dandelions. I turned to Jay and said, "I want to make sure I don't make the same mistakes I made last time."

"Tell me more about that," Jay said, smiling at me, his hands full of dandelions.

"Well, I want to make sure we never end up in the same rut Nick and I did. I've learned my lesson the hard way, you know? I want to make sure we have clear priorities, that we put the right things first." I smiled back, sincerely. "What do you think about taking some time to talk about what each of us wants?" I knew Jay would be up for it.

During the rest of that weekend, we sat down and hammered out our priorities, our boundaries, and our values. There were so many things we agreed on, so many similarities for what we wanted out of life, it was almost unbelievable. Our list was long, and we knew it would have to be a little flexible as we continued to grow as individuals and as a couple, but we were happy with our starting point.

Vacations were just one of the things we'd firmly decided we would make time for. Jay's love of adventure merged perfectly with my intense desire to make the most of every moment. "Staycations" were a bit easier with a little one so at first we just took a couple fun weekends away—one at an incredible little Puget Sound resort and one on a little road trip for a weekend in Portland. Then, in October Jay spontaneously suggested and subsequently set up an international trip! First we would visit my incredible friend Dawn Green in London, who I'd originally met through the appendix cancer Facebook support group. Then Jay and I would take the Eurostar on to Paris. *Ooh la la*, was I absolutely over the moon!

Jay's mom had special access to airline passes from her years as a flight attendant, which made the impulse trip financially feasible. As it turned out, flying on family passes didn't just mean cheap tickets, it meant flying standby—and flying standby meant being flexible. On our flight to Heathrow Airport in London we were given a last-minute first-class upgrade, complete with bottomless champagne, a five-course meal, and fully reclining bed chairs. After a mostly romantic trip with just a few hiccups, on the way back to Seattle we found ourselves stranded in a rundown motel in Atlanta with moist sheets, hair in the sink, and what I'm pretty sure was mold growing on the nightstand.

Just like flying standby, learning to love a new person meant appreciating the perks *and* getting past the downsides. Simply put, just like life in general, life with Jay wasn't *all* a fairy tale. There was first class and no class, romantic date nights and toddler potty accidents. There were beautiful conversations where I felt completely heard and a number of arguments where I was certain he would never understand. But the perks and the downsides helped me see even more clearly the ways we complemented each other.

Jay was meant to be my second chapter. Not a plan B, but more like a plan A-2, in no way less than what came before. Together we were creating something just as amazing, although entirely different.

Jay made his intentions quite clear early on in our relationship. "Just so you know, I'm not dating you for fun. I asked you out because I can see this going beyond just boyfriend and girlfriend."

I had smiled as he pulled me close. I was down for that. Fooling around was for the birds. At least, it certainly wasn't for me.

I knew our engagement might be somewhere on the horizon, but I didn't focus too much on that. My practice of living mindfully in the moment was still in full swing, and I was very much enjoying getting to know and learning how to love my boyfriend.

By December 14, Jay and I had been dating for five months exactly. *Knock, knock, knock.* I jumped off the floor where I was playing with Austyn and practically ran to the door. We were going out, and as he often did, Jay had kept the location for our date night a surprise. I did know we were going somewhere cold. I'd pulled a pair of my favorite jeans over a pair of leggings, when he'd called last minute, warning me to "dress warm." My dad was already over to watch Austyn for the evening.

"Hey, Jay Bae-Bae!" I opened the front door laughing and using the nickname I always sang out as if I were in a Chris Hurricane music video.

After giving my dad a hug and Austyn extra loves, I practically skipped out the door Jay opened for me as always. For the entire thirty-minute drive, I tried to guess where we were going. I didn't get it right until we pulled into Bellevue Park on the Eastside. Every year at Christmastime, they plopped an ice-skating rink right in the middle of the city park, tucked between little boutiques and huge skyscrapers. I was thrilled as I'd always wanted to go.

We skated for nearly an hour, spinning around to Christmas music and trying really hard not to run over any kids. I couldn't help but smile the entire time. I couldn't believe I'd gotten lucky enough to have two insanely amazing men to love. I knew for certain it was less luck and more created opportunity though. I'd chosen to partner with my Creator and allow Him to make good come from some of the worst things in my life. Somehow that had led to this.

Once I'd pulled my skates off and rubbed my sore ankles, I shoved my feet into my winter boots. Jay offered me a hand up, we turned in our skates, and he pulled me toward the exit.

"Where are we going?"

"I made us reservations because I knew you would be starving!" Jay winked as he said it. He really did know me well.

Telling Jay about my latest challenge with Austyn's stubborn refusal to potty-train, I recounted the horrible mess all over my bathroom that afternoon. I lengthened my stride and tried to pick up the pace as I laughed about the "doody" debacle of the century. Just as I started getting to the really good part, Jay stopped.

"What are you doing?" I asked, trying to pull him along. "C'mon, babe! I'm hungry!" But he didn't budge.

"Look!" Jay said, blushing and pointing up, "Mistletoe!"

Before I could think twice about why on earth mistletoe would be hanging from a branch on a tree in the middle of a city park, I locked my arms around his neck, stood on my toes and kissed him unreservedly. Whether we'd just been talking about poop or potpourri, I always felt free to be myself in his embrace. I felt blissful, confident. So sure of *us*. It was as if I could see our future. No, not every detail, but I knew big things were in store. This whole partnering up with God thing was great. I felt like I could trust God—and my gut—better than ever before. I knew without a doubt I would cherish this night for the rest of my life.

When I pulled away, Jay leaned in again. I thought he wanted another kiss, but then I realized he was grabbing something out of the tree behind me.

My hands flew over my mouth as Jay got down on one knee, a small box in his hand.

"Alyssa," he said. "You have made me so incredibly happy these last five months, and I'm ready to take care of you and Austyn. I want to love you for the rest of our lives and make every day an adventure with you." His voice was shaking as he opened the box and a diamond solitaire engagement ring sparkled brightly in the darkness. "Will you marry me?"

"Oh, my goodness! *Yes!*" I shouted and bent over to kiss his smiling face. I only stopped jumping long enough for him to slip the ring on my finger. I was suddenly aware there'd been someone strumming a guitar and singing one of my favorite Christmas songs somewhere nearby. I couldn't stop bouncing; it felt like a perfect moment, my own little miracle! Tears glistened in the corners of my eyes, threatening to spill over.

"How did you plan all this?" I squealed. Just then I noticed the guy with the guitar walking toward us was my friend Sean, who happens to be an incredible musician and was the lead violinist in one of my favorite bands since high school.

"Congratulations!" His wife, one of my best friends, Cat, emerged, beaming.

Jay knew how much I cherished their incredible friendship. Just as I was about to cry from seeing two of my favorites, two more of our closest friends surprised me. Jacki, who was like a sister to Jay, growing up in the same cul-de-sac, and her boyfriend, Andy. I gave everyone hugs and showed the girls my ring as the guys thumped Jay on the back. I danced on my feet, my voice uncontrollably squeaky as I tried to put it all together. *How in the world had he pulled this off?*

In true Jay fashion, he had been planning the romantic event for weeks. He'd asked my dad for permission over a month before and my dad had happy-cried his agreement. The diamond wasn't just sparkly, it had extra significance as it was his mother's diamond from her own ring. He'd gone to great lengths to plan the ice skating, the walk to the park, the well-placed mistletoe, and the lighted ring box. He'd recruited our friends to take pictures, record a video, and place the ring in the tree just before we got into the courtyard. It couldn't have been more perfect for me if he tried.

"And, that's not all. Jay had us bring your favorite!" Jacki held up a bottle of my favorite champagne and six plastic flutes—perfect for the park. I held onto Jay as he popped the cork under the sparkling Christmas lights.

Everyone cheered, "To Jay and Alyssa!" and clinked glasses. It was perfect. I felt like I was living out the conclusion to a Nicolas Sparks novel. I knew I'd remember every single detail for as long as I lived—even the preproposal poop chat and the postproposal prosecco cheers.

And we hadn't even had dinner yet!

Jay and I decided we were ready to put down some roots together. Another milestone meant another opportunity for me to pull my "brave pants" up really high. When I felt like I was going to hyperventilate at the mention of *buying* a house, Jay and I talked through the reasons it made sense financially. When I felt like I was going to throw up when we actually looked at a property, Jay walked me through it all again. This time he made sure to touch on the fact that we could sell the house if we ever needed to.

As much as I'd come to love my place in Seattle, after a simple conversation we knew we wanted to settle down and raise Austyn outside of the city. After eyeing a few houses in the surrounding suburbs, I stuffed down the vomity feeling long enough to fall in love when we visited a building site in my childhood hometown just north of Seattle. My ever-deepening relationship with God was giving me more certainty. I swear the more I exercised my courage, the more I felt bravery becoming a part of who I was.

"Let's make an offer!" I'd said to Jay earlier that day, bouncing up and down with excitement, trying hard not to pee my pants (I'm a mom, don't blame me). Jay had whooped his agreement and pulled me in for a kiss. The butterflies kicked up again.

We had the pick of the lots and we chose one on a slope, tucked up next to a beautiful forest. I could already picture our little future home there, brimming over with love, on land with woods that reminded me of where I grew up.

My bestie/realtor submitted the offer for us that day.

"Guess what, beautiful?" Jay was smiling wide as he got off the phone in the kitchen at my Green Lake house a few hours later. "They accepted the offer!"

"What? No way!" I squealed and broke out in a happy dance. Austyn raced into the room, curious about the commotion, and I picked her up, swinging her around with tears in my eyes. "Thank you, God!"

One miracle after another, my life was shifting in so many ways, and so quickly it almost felt unreal. It hadn't been that long ago that I'd felt completely lost, angry at the world, and unsure if I believed in love or hope or God at all. I hadn't been sure of *where* I would live or if I even *wanted to*. Then I found my infinite hope. I'd discovered incredible trust. And if that wasn't enough (it was), now almost every single other detail was falling together. I knew it was, in part, because I believed they could. I knew trusting God did not guarantee rainbows and butterflies, in fact quite the opposite, but I was determined to soak up all the good coming my way while I could.

I remembered Job and felt like I was living a modern-day version of his story in the Bible. I'd lost so much. My health. My first baby. My incredible husband. Then I'd moved away from my house, my friends, and my family. I'd turned my back on my faith and even felt like I'd lost my future. Then God had challenged me to trust Him despite my circumstances just as He challenged Job in the Bible. Regardless of all the ways I'd previously renounced Him, doubted Him, and straight-up blamed Him for my suffering, I now had *almost* all of what I lost back after I chose to trust Him again. It was not in the way I might have guessed, or in the way I would have chosen if it were up to me. But He'd literally turned my chaos into courage, my grief into joy, and my loss into love.

As these new blessings began to unfold, voices in my head told me how little I deserved them. Instead of listening, I tried trusting and accepting the goodness I'd received as a generous gift. I thanked God for every grace and marveled at His handiwork.

Somehow my Creator had worked it all together so the impossible was becoming possible. I was in awe that I had dared God to make good of my tragedy, and He had done just that. Then I remembered how years before, I had doubted God could work in the life of someone like Jay. Funny how things turn out.

Touché, God, touché.

Chapter EIGHTEEN

Now I Know
We Have a Hand in Our
Destiny

BETWEEN PLANNING FOR THE wedding, working with designers on the new house, attempting to potty-train Austyn (picture wrestling an angry octopus into a vase because that's *exactly* how easy it is to potty-train a strong-willed toddler), and writing to keep my business afloat, I was *the* definition of what you call a hot mess. At least I was a happy hot mess although still far from healthy.

After kicking my morning off with yet another failed attempt to skip the Starbucks drive-through and actually make a healthy breakfast, I came across a Facebook post from Jay's good friend, Jacki. What caught my eye was the energy she said she'd gained from changing her lifestyle. When I first looked into what this healthy lifestyle thing *actually* entailed, I was intrigued. Basically, women did daily workouts, checked into online groups for accountability, and helped support each other on the quest to eat right. It sounded good to me, *especially* the accountability part since I couldn't stick to my routine for crap. Then I read more. The workouts were to be done mostly from home, and then there were the shakes these girls all apparently drank. I was wildly skeptical about both. All of *that* sounded like something my mother would have done . . . back in the eighties . . . while wearing a neon spandex leotard. *No thanks!*

But when Jay found out I was considering it, he put in his two cents. "You've tried everything else. Why wouldn't you try it and see if it helps your energy? Or your disease? You said there's a money-back guarantee, right?"

Despite my skepticism, I knew he was right. I might as well exercise my "brave muscle" again and do the thing that scared me. Just to see.

So I dove in and did my best, which was humbling to say the least. I thought the workouts would be easy for an ex-college soccer player. But I had to modify every single one of those moves. And when I started tracking my food for the meal planning, I realized I had been making so many allowances for what I'd been eating that I wasn't nourishing my body the way I knew I was supposed to from all my studies when Nick was sick.

Fast forward a few weeks and I'd started to get the hang of everything. I still couldn't do a lunge to save my life and push-ups on my toes were out of the question. But I noticed my digestion was finally back on track, and my energy was up toward the end of the day.

After a few months when I went in for my wedding dress alterations, I was surprised to find I'd also dropped two dress sizes! The women in the boutique wanted to know what I had been doing to get in such great shape. I was actually pretty impressed myself! All of the hard work and the accountability to actually do it was paying off!

My friends and family even started commenting on the change in my demeanor and pants size. I was flattered by the compliments and swiftly sent all interested parties on to Jacki. That's when she suggested, "You should start your own group! You'd be a great coach!"

"Thanks, but no thanks. That's definitely not my thing." I was a busy and for a-little-while-longer-still a single mom with absolutely no formal training in fitness. I didn't think I had the time to do something on the side. "But sign me up for *your* groups for life," I said.

For the first time in my adult life, the new structure in my mornings provided the perfect foundation for me to spend regular time with my Creator before the day began. I was getting up an hour before Austyn, crushing a workout, and getting closer to God—all before I used to roll out of bed! It honestly felt like God had led me right to the missing puzzle piece for my health, so that I actually had time and energy to live on purpose.

"Hey! It's been a while since you've said anything about your neck or your glands," Jay commented one day after work. It took us a minute to connect the dots. But sure enough, my symptoms had all but gone away after six weeks. This lifestyle shift was clearly making a difference, and I was beyond thrilled! I could barely believe it. My back even seemed to be healing itself after I had struggled with back pain for years after a car accident. Starting to treat myself better physically than I had in a very, *very* long time was pulling so many loose ends of my life together. I was actually feeling good . . . mind, soul, and . . . *finally*, body.

Sitting down at my computer one morning after dropping Austyn off at preschool, I pulled up my latest writing project and sighed. I was working on a series of blog posts for an old school tattoo makeup boutique. While grateful for the work, convincing women to get tattooed lip liner wasn't my thing, and it was absolutely soul-sucking to have to fake it.

In my heart, I wanted to help people, especially women, see their inherent worth, not just encourage them to draw attention to their fleeting beauty. I wanted to tangibly make a difference by helping people dig deep and see past their current circumstances to find their true potential in life. While I knew my clients appreciated the words I strung together for them, I finally realized it was time to make that career move I'd been thinking about for months. I finally had the energy to do something to make my way out of this profession and into one where I could make the kind of impact I wanted to make in the world—a lasting one.

Pastor Eric's words from our conversation months prior came to mind, "Have you ever thought of becoming a life coach?"

I didn't even know what life coaches did and wondered who would trust me to teach them.

Pastor Eric had said, "You might not see it, Alyssa, but you have a lot to offer people. You have wisdom beyond your years. Most people don't know how to survive the things you've gone through—let alone thrive through them." Before we finished our conversation, he'd added, "I think it's something you need to look into. I feel like you are supposed to be helping people find the kind of peace you've found in your life. Just think about it."

Not even ten minutes after I was done with my lip liner work for the day, I applied at a Seattle life-coaching school. Immediately after that, I messaged Jacki, asking for more information on their coaching programs and training. I would need as much help as I could get. And, I knew she and the larger community she was a part of had business-building tools and all the know-how. From what I could tell, all I had to do as a coach with them was start an accountability group of my own, stay on my own health journey, and help other women start theirs. It was an easy decision because I was already hooked on the whole becoming-the-best-version-of-myself thing.

I didn't know what I was doing at first, but in true entrepreneurial fashion, I kept going anyway. I ended up leaning away from the traditional schooling and instead taught myself, attended free trainings, learned from my coach, and watched as many YouTube videos as I could while putting it all into practice and failing my way through it. My professional attention slowly shifted from contract work and copywriting to crafting content for my *own* business. Eventually, I dubbed our brand Made for Brave Coaching and was thrilled to be able to focus on mind, body, and soul health with our clients in online monthly accountability groups.

At first I helped just a few brave souls, but we grew very quickly and were in the black before I knew it. I'd always loved a good online business model—flexibility and low overhead costs can't be beat. Good business sense aside, I was truly humbled every day I got to walk alongside such incredible women. I couldn't believe just how fulfilling most, if not all, of the daily work felt. The more lives our team impacted, the more my income grew, and I began dropping my writing contracts one by one.

Coaching meant I got to write about things that mattered. It meant I had an opportunity to get close to women, to share my struggles and discoveries, and encourage them to start really diving into what mattered to them. I finally felt like I found my perfect fit.

I tore open the padded envelope I'd gotten from my mailbox, postmarked all the way from the UK, and a note fell to the counter. *Dear Alyssa, I wanted to send this to you. Your something blue. I love you, and I can't wait to see you in Seattle soon! XO. Dawn*

Inside the envelope was a jewelry pouch with a glimmering Tiffany-blue opal necklace inside. I called her right away.

"Dawn, it's perfect! I love it! Thank you so much!"

"I'm so glad you do! I thought it was beautiful, and it reminded me of you. Shining so brightly. I'm so proud of you and the work you are doing, darling."

I could hear the beaming smile in Dawn's voice through the phone. "I wanted to make sure you got it before your big day, just in case you don't like it, so you can get something else if you need to."

It was still morning in Seattle but nearing bedtime in Kettering where she lived in the countryside, just a train ride from London. I pictured Dawn in her apartment snuggled up with her sweet pup, where Jay and I had stayed with her on our trip just about six months before.

"I absolutely love it. Thank you!" We talked for over an hour about how she'd been managing with her disease, about my new business, and her plans to join our fit tribe. We connected as often as we could via phone and text. Dawn and I had become so very close over the years. She'd been fighting appendix cancer for almost a decade while simultaneously creating and leading an incredible nonprofit to help others who were also affected by this horrible disease. Superwoman, basically. I looked up to her so very much.

A couple of weeks after that call, just six weeks before Dawn's flight was scheduled to take off for Seattle, I got a message from a mutual friend of ours in the UK. Her seat on the plane and her place at our wedding would be empty.

I wept for days.

With our big day fast approaching, I was excited for our June wedding but also looking forward to having the whole thing behind us. Planning a wedding with a three-year-old in tow while launching a new business and slowly dissolving another at the same time was an undertaking of epic proportions. I was thankful to be feeling incredible energy-wise and had even been able to wean myself off the steroids without so much as a hint of my disease making a reappearance. I was ready!

In what felt like the last sprint of a very long marathon, we dialed in the plans for our honeymoon, put the finishing touches on our favors, and hired a babysitter to be on location with us on the big day.

Just when we thought we'd hit a calm spot, we got the phone call saying it was time to officially close on our finally finished house. The rental agreement on my place in Green Lake was just about up, so the timing was perfect, albeit just a bit chaotic.

"Congratulations, you guys!" Meg, my realtor and friend, said as she handed over the keys to our new home. I couldn't believe the months of design consultations and construction snafus had finally come to an end. Talk about starting another life chapter; this felt like an entirely different book with a new me, new home, and a new marriage.

Stepping through the front door with my soon-to-be husband on move-in day, I was hit with an overwhelming sense of gratitude. With happy tears forming in my eyes, I felt something shift inside me. I heard a promise whispered right into my heart. It was as if God was saying, *I'm not anywhere near finished yet*, which just made me cry harder. I couldn't stop the gratitude from pouring from my lips. *Thank You. Thank You. Thank You!*

After the movers unloaded all of our furniture and boxes, Jay wanted to make a run to the grocery store to stock the fridge before my mom dropped Austyn off in an hour. I'm telling you, this guy is a keeper! Food first, unpack later. Priorities on point!

"I'll be right back," he said, adding, "I love you, beautiful."

"I love you more."

"I love you most."

"I love you always."

As he pulled his car out of the driveway, I wandered upstairs, walking from room to room, reveling in it all. I was in awe. I was euphoric. Falling to my knees in the corner of what would become Austyn's bedroom, I thanked God again for His provision, in complete awe of what my Maker had done.

Then I was struck with a sudden realization that this house, though quite a bit smaller, had just as many bedrooms as the house Nick and I first bought together. A stab of pain shot through my chest. Nick and I had planned to fill our home with love and dreamed of filling those bedrooms with children. But that house had turned out to be a place of complete and utter loss, an empty shell of the life I'd imagined.

Yet here I was starting over. Dreaming again. *What if I face the same nightmare here?* For a moment, I took my eyes off of God and felt overcome with fear. I was getting ready to promise "till death do us part," and death could very well be right around the corner.

My future with Jay looked bright. We wanted kids. We wanted to impact lives together in a way we hoped would point people to God. Those were the things we wished for, but we had no clue how they would all pan out. I couldn't pretend I knew what the future held as I already knew the truth. I had lived it. *Nothing is promised.*

Putting my head between my knees, I allowed my mind to spiral for a solid five minutes. Then I wiped away my tears and forced myself to stop. I knew the spiral was pointless. The worry was unwarranted. I no longer had to be afraid. I was loved by the Ruler of every atom in the universe.

"Take my plans, God. Take my dreams. Take my life. Take my future. I'm surrendering them all to You . . . again." I had to make the decision daily to recommit my life, my faith, and my future to God. Every time

I did, it just seemed to get a little bit easier. I never imagined surrender could be so sweet.

After I poured out my heart, I still had no idea what the future held, but the tension in my shoulders was gone, and I found myself skipping back down the hall with a smile on my face. Nothing was wrong, and I should start acting like it. I would focus on living in the present every time I felt as if I might drown in anxiety over the future. I didn't have to let myself sink. We weren't made to get caught up in the past or float ahead in the future, which is why we feel so badly when we allow ourselves to do that. We are made to live bravely and gratefully in the present.

June 25, 2016, went down in history as one of the very best days of my life. Under a hot, bright sun, with our family and friends surrounding us, I married my best friend . . . for the second time.

Pastor Eric was our officiant on the attractively landscaped estate with a view of the Cascade Mountains behind us, where the wedding took place. He brought tears to our eyes as he spoke of how the love of God heals our brokenness.

Jay kissed me at the altar the same way he had on my porch not even a year before. As we walked back down the aisle together, arms behind each other's backs, both crying happy tears, I could barely believe we were now husband and wife.

The reception was held in a barn on the estate where 150 guests gathered to celebrate under café lights. It was so hot that beads of sweat ran down my back, but there was nothing that could keep the smile off my face.

Just as we sat down to eat, I watched Austyn sneak off behind her babysitter's back and stuff several brownies into her mouth at once, dripping gooey chocolate all over her face. I found myself laughing out loud when she approached our table in all her toddler glory with her chocolate-smeared white dress, insisting she'd only had, "One bite, Mom!"

I had worried about so many little things at my first wedding. But this time around, I felt blissful. I felt free.

The person I was on that day was not the same me I was when I said "I do" to Nick. In every way, I had become a different version of the person I had been eight years before. My vows meant something different to me too. In a way, they meant more. Knowing what "till death do us part" could entail made it real. I knew what I was committing to, and it wasn't for the faint of heart.

My family, Jay's family, and Nick's family all were there. Friends from both my former life and this new one all came to celebrate with us. I stroked the ring on my right hand, my last gift from Nick, and touched the blue opal from Dawn I'd attached to my bouquet. I knew the loved ones we'd lost were there with us too.

I held Austyn in my lap during the toasts, squeezing her tight in between bites of cake. "Goosey! Do you know what today is?" I asked.

"Umm-hmm," she nodded, licking another bit of frosting off her plate. "Our wedding day!" She smiled her big beautiful smile that so resembled Nick's, and my heart about melted right then and there. "I love Mommy and Daddy Day!" She still couldn't say Jay's name quite right, but we rarely corrected her because it was entirely too cute.

It was all I could to do keep from ugly, grateful crying all over her in that moment and again during my first dance with Jay. When I finally danced with my dad, all bets were off. Nick was smiling down on us, I was certain. I could almost hear him celebrating with God as our Creator revealed things to Nick I still hadn't even experienced, little surprises He still had in store.

My journey with grief and hardship was far from over. But I also knew, without a doubt, God's got it. And He had clearly "had it" all along.

Chapter NINETEEN

Now I Know Triumph Can Come from Tragedy

MOST PEOPLE WERE 100 percent on board when Jay and I started dating, including Nick's family. But it was disconcerting when a couple of people (mostly online) seemed to have a serious problem when I actually got *remarried*. Especially when I got remarried and seemed happy about it. Apparently, at twenty-six years of age I was supposed to remain single and in mourning for the rest of my life.

The messages I got aren't worth repeating; many were more vile than you could imagine, and all were based on untrue assumptions and judgments.

Almost all (like 99.9 percent) of the emails, cards, messages, and comments that I got and get to this day are so incredibly positive. I cherish every one of those encouraging responses and hang the physical notes, letters, and cards on the wall in my office to remind me it's worth it to keep showing up, to keep being brave. I save them to remind myself there might be one more family or one more person out there who needs to know they aren't alone.

Before going through all this, I could have easily been one of my accusers. (Okay, not online. I would never spread negativity that way against people I don't even know.) But let me give you an example of the Judgey-McJudgerson I used to be.

I met a widower through work a couple of years after his wife passed away. When he told me he was about to get remarried, I was sick to my stomach at the thought. This was months before Nick's stomach started hurting, and he was still in his healthy-as-a-horse phase with no hint of anything gone wrong. I remember feeling disgust at how quickly it seemed like my new work friend had moved on and thinking I could never do such a thing. I didn't say it out loud, but internally I judged my new friend and the depth of love he had with his first wife. I now see just how ridiculous it was for me to judge another human being on his life experience when *I* hadn't experienced anything like it myself. Shame on me.

It's interesting the contradictions we hold as a culture. After my miscarriage, not one person asked me if I was sure I could love another baby while simultaneously loving and grieving the baby I'd lost. When a mother loses a child, nobody ever questions her capacity to love her other children and the one she's lost, equally but differently. When a mother has two or three or even six babies, nobody wonders if she can love her kids enough just because she has more than one. Why is it so hard to believe a person's heart can expand to love another spouse while still holding space for their first? I'm convinced it's simply a lack of understanding and an unwillingness to even try.

Of course, I still grieve. Of course, I still find myself attempting to shield my heart from further bruising. Of course, I still miss Nick—extremely. But, in many ways, I feel it is because of my loss that

I am able to love in a deeper, more intimate way. I'd learned so many lessons during the first twenty-eight years of my life that I knew a little bit more about what to appreciate and what I could let slide.

Jay and I worked hard to keep our priorities straight in our relationship *because* of the way I'd messed up a couple of my precious years with Nick. We made time with each other and our family a nonnegotiable despite our increasingly busy lives. When my business picked up even more, we created room for even more intentional time together as a couple and as a family. We made "no phone zones" during certain hours of our day a top priority.

We knew we would need to be mindful if we wanted to build an exceptional marriage. The same was true for me if I wanted to get closer to the version of the person I was made to be. I would have to do it on purpose. I had to constantly work at focusing on truth and banishing that nasty little voice inside my head that tells me, *You will never be enough.* Instead I repeated the truth: "God is always enough."

After our wedding and honeymoon in Hawaii, Jay and I made sure we kept our relationship at the top of our priority lists. We found ourselves geeking out over working toward a better version of ourselves. We kept up with our morning quiet times with God, our date nights with each other, working out, and eating right. My job as an online accountability coach made all those things even easier to stick to as we were surrounded by other people doing the same things.

All those superfoods and date nights must have done something for us, because Jay and I found out we were pregnant just a few months into our marriage. It was late September and the leaves were glowing brightly. With my health firmly intact, a baby on the way, and the online business booming, the world was positively bouncing with possibility.

Shortly after our nuptials, Jay told me he wanted to take the necessary steps to legally adopt Austyn. I broke down in joyful tears when he said he wanted to be her dad in every sense of the word—no question. The idea of adoption had always been close to my heart. Knowing my little girl would have a planet-bound dad again was almost too much to handle.

Jay decided to file *pro se* (he would represent himself, without an attorney), which meant we had to learn all the ins and outs of Washington State adoptions. There were forms to fill out, home studies to conduct, case workers to contact, background checks to complete, and a battery of live interviews to do. Months later, we would *finally* have our court date to go before a judge and make it legal.

"Do you promise you'll love her as your own?" the judge asked him. "You realize this isn't a just-until-she's-eighteen thing, right?" This judge was clearly experienced, and I wondered what kind of cases had come through his courtroom over the years. "Even when she drops out of college and comes back home or needs money to make rent. I mean, I'm not saying those things will happen, I'm just saying, this is for life. You'll be responsible for her. No matter what happens to your wife. No matter how many times your little girl says she hates you as a teenager. And believe me, I have my own girls; she will say it." The judge smiled but was very serious. "No matter what, you'll be her dad. Always. Are you sure that's what you want?" he asked, looking Jay dead in the eye.

"Yes, sir." Jay had been nodding his head the whole time, shoulders squared. But I saw the glimmer of a tear in his eye as a contented smile played across his face. "It would be my honor."

When we left the courtroom, documents in hand, an officially official family, all three of us were practically skipping. When we had our picture taken in front of the courthouse that day, our smiles were huge, and you could already see the beginning of my little baby bump.

But just when I thought things couldn't get any better, I started bleeding. At first I was in denial, but the cramps that followed a horrific conversation with my doctor turned into contractions the next day. Our sweet baby went to heaven. My second child lost to miscarriage. The pain was almost too much to bear.

That night, my tears fell hard as I lay in front of the fireplace in our new house, letting the heat from the fire soothe my aching back. Jay sat beside me on the floor, gently stroking my hair as I sobbed through until morning.

It took me weeks to recover physically and longer to recover emotionally. But after the worst of it had passed, I looked at myself in the mirror and didn't hate the person in my reflection. The first time around, I had despised myself and loathed my body for failing my baby. This time I looked at my physical form with lots of love and lots of grace.

I did soothing workouts, I checked in with our fit family who were incredibly supportive through our loss, and I ate for the nourishment of my body and my soul. The biggest difference was that I was finally trusting God in the middle of my storm. After all, we were best friends these days. He never said we wouldn't experience hardship, but He did tell us we don't have to climb our mountains alone. Although I didn't understand how He could work this hard part out for good just yet, I trusted if anyone could do it, He could. I gave the precious little life and yet another big loss to Him.

"You know what helps me?" I said to Jay one night after a few months had passed. We were cuddled up in bed getting ready for sleep, Jay lovingly rubbing my back.

Jay and I were already doing so much better communicating in our marriage than Nick and I had early on. Mainly, because we did it on purpose, almost every single night. I was so used to sharing anything and everything with Jay at the end of his busy work day that it was a reflex now. I never even thought of keeping anything important to myself, even if my feelings were complicated.

"What helps, beautiful?" Jay asked.

"It helps me to know that Nick is up in heaven, taking care of our baby. And that the first baby Nick and I lost is probably friends with our little one too. They're siblings, you know?" I smiled as a tear slipped down my cheek. "And down here, we get to take care of Austyn, while he takes care of our kid. It's kind of cool to think, right?"

I never had to hesitate about bringing up Nick to Jay if he was on my heart. At first, we'd had to work through a few things with our counselor in that regard. But once Jay realized the love I would always hold for Nick would never again compete with the love I held for him, things got a lot easier. Losing the baby hit Jay hard too, but just like Nick, his faith never wavered.

"I hadn't thought about it like that before. You're right." His smile reached all the way to his ever-beautiful blue eyes, crinkling them at the corner. "That *is* pretty cool."

I nuzzled my face into the crook of his shoulder as he squeezed me in closer, kissing the top of my head. This guy of mine, *my second first*. I couldn't believe all the challenges we'd already endured. I'd been finding myself falling more and more in love with my husband and his quiet strength every single day. And, walking through the hard stuff with him was just proving it to me over again... God knew what He was doing with my second chapter. Jay was truly my perfect match.

Through this new hurt, I feel myself getting even closer to God too as He continued to move in my heart. I was being vulnerable in my posts on social media and in my blog, in hopes that sharing showed other women they weren't alone. And I kept meeting women I could relate to who said they could relate to me. I felt beautifully broken but wholly in process. Like a cracked vase, I knew God was putting me back together yet again. But this time, I'd be even stronger . . . all for His glory.

Jay fell asleep as I lay quietly awake staring up at the ceiling that night, counting and recounting my blessings. Then I asked God to do what He knew was best. I had learned to trust Him with even the big things now. When Jay and I first got married, I had prayed for a baby. But now I prayed for *His will* for our family, whatever that looked like, bundle of joy or not.

"Mom, when will we get a baby?" Austyn looked up at me one day, her big, blue eyes searching mine. She had started to beg Jay and me for a sibling almost immediately after our wedding. She didn't know anything about the one we'd already lost.

"I'm not sure, sweet girl." I squeezed her tight, taking in her innocent, flawless face while trying not to cry.

"Well, let's go to the store and *get one!*" she said, with a sincere grin and a shrug of her shoulders.

I sighed. "Oh, Goosey. That's not how it works."

"How does it work then?"

I thought for a moment. How to answer this question for a three-year-old? "We have to pray for one." It was true. Well, that and one other thing.

It's not like we hadn't been trying. We had been for months, to no avail. The doctor had even thrown around the idea of fertility treatments. At almost thirty, I was apparently on the verge of being geriatric in terms of fertility. But Jay and I chose to discuss adoption as an option instead as there were so many babies out there who needed love. I'd worked so hard to get off all of my medications, there was no way I would go back to a chemically-dependent life now.

"Okay, Momma. I'm going to pray right now then. Close your eyes!" Austyn folded her hands in her lap and watched until I obeyed her instruction.

My tears threatened to spill as she began.

"Dear Jesus. Please help Mommy to get a baby in her tummy. Because I really want a baby. We love You, God." She ended every prayer with her customary closing, "Amen, forever and ever."

"There!" She smiled big and threw her tiny arms around my waist. "Now we will get a baby because we prayed for one," she pronounced and went right back to her play.

She had such determined assurance that I almost believed her. Her childlike faith reminded me in that moment of how far I had to go. Faith is never a destination; it's a daily decision, one I might have been subconsciously "forgetting" to commit to yet again. Oh how fragile are our hearts that shy away from love and hope for fear of being let down.

As I continued to give all areas of life my best, including my work, Made for Brave Coaching flourished. By April of 2017, not even a year after our wedding, Jay left his full-time corporate job to partner with me in our Made for Brave Coaching business. It wasn't long before I couldn't even fathom trying to do it without him.

Owning and operating a business together as a newly married couple wasn't an easy feat. We went through quite a few ups and downs in those first months. But by summer, we'd mostly worked through the kinks by playing to our individual strengths and defining what roles and responsibilities each of us "owned." We figured out what each of us loved and tried to split up the rest. Once we found our groove, I was amazed how well we worked together in all areas. Jay leaned in to help with the housework just as much as the business stuff, and we truly became partners in every area of life, as I believe it should be. What we were doing together felt so much more complete than what we might have done apart.

In the weeks before we were to leave for our first big coaching conference, any spare minutes had been devoted to researching adoption. We'd been exploring for months and praying about options. But I'd fallen back into old patterns and had been failing miserably at letting God take the lead in this area. I hadn't felt His express hand in the matter, but I kept pushing forward anyway. I figured I would go, go, go until He explicitly said, "No, no, no!"

The day before our flight left for the conference, we were scheduled for another virtual meeting with an adoption agency we loved that was based out of California. Right after that video call, we were to send in our first hefty down payment. We'd already done a number of consultations with them, and I was anxious to finally be moving forward. Right before the meeting was about to start, I felt the distinct nudge to move the appointment to *after* the trip. I emailed the receptionist to reschedule for the day after our return. I was bummed but knew five days wouldn't make much of a difference.

"That was incredible! What do you want to implement first?" Jay asked from the driver's seat on the way home. We couldn't stop talking about all the things we'd learned. But I was feeling so tired I wasn't sure I could manage.

"I'm not sure, babe! I'm just as excited as you, but whatever we do, I need a nap first." I'd been exhausted the entire trip. My newfound energy was one of my most valued qualities, so I noticed immediately when it began to plummet. For a split second, I feared my autoimmune disease had returned.

"You're probably just jet-lagged," Jay offered. "First, *all* the naps . . . then, we crush it!" He smiled and reached over to take my hand, bringing it up to his mouth for a kiss.

The next morning, on a complete whim, I took an at-home pregnancy test. Right before my eyes, hours before our rescheduled adoption appointment, a tiny pink line appeared. We were pregnant! I was thrilled!

On a sunny Pacific Northwest day in August of 2017, Jay and I pulled into our garage after a visit to the doctor. "Let's tell her!" Jay was practically giddy, and I couldn't help but give in and join him in his joy. I leaned over and hugged him with tears in my eyes. I could barely believe it. Eight months after our miscarriage and eight months since Austyn started praying, I was holding a small, white envelope with an ultrasound photo. We'd just seen the heartbeat of our rainbow baby, a perfect little seven-weeks-along miracle!

Sitting Austyn down on the back porch as my dad filmed, I said, "Guess what, Goosey? There's a baby in mommy's tummy!" Her reaction was everything.[3]

---

3   Austyn's reaction to hearing the news of the baby on video: madeforbrave.com/babybrave.

Chapter TWENTY

Now I Know Bravery Lies Just Beyond the Fear

ON THE DAY WE told Austyn about the pregnancy, she squealed, "I get a baby sister!" We made sure she knew the chances were just as high for a brother. But as it turned out, she was absolutely right!

Baby Brave, as we called her, was a girl! What began as a list of over ninety-five potential baby names was immediately cut down to about sixty when we found out her gender. I was specifically drawn to the ones that began with the letter E, but the only name I really *loved* got a hard *no* from Jay. In a lot of smaller issues, his answer was usually, "Whatever you'd like, beautiful." Sometimes I had to pry an opinion out of him, but not for something as important as this.

We'd been at a standstill on names for almost an entire twenty-four hours when my handsome-as-heck hubby suggested one I hadn't heard before. The two of us were in the car waiting for a ferry to take us to one of the San Juan Islands for what people call a "babymoon."

"Oh my goodness," I exclaimed. "I actually think I love it!" I whipped out my phone to look up the meaning. Once my Google search loaded, I turned to face Jay in my seat as happy tears welled up in my eyes.

"It's *perfect!*" I told him what the name meant and his jaw dropped. With shining eyes, he pulled me in for a long hug, and I basked in the bliss.

It was crazy to think of all the times we'd put our two heads together over the course of the last two and a half years to come up with solutions. Whether it was how to get puke stains out of the carpet when Austyn came down with the flu after eating an entire bowl of raspberries, or figuring out the best way to take care of payroll now that we'd hired an assistant to help with our business, we were simply better together. How fitting that we'd come up with our little girl's name together too.

Austyn's unique energy, smile, and zest for life are the first things most people notice about her. She's always been all about the action but incredibly compassionate too. That's just one part of why Jay is the perfect match for us. Almost every night the two of them have an intense pillow fight that would send most people running for the hills. Austyn loves it and squeals with joy and laughter at the challenge of trying to knock Jay's hat off his head.

One night just before her bedtime, I was doing the dishes and the two of them were pummeling each other as they do. When it suddenly got quiet, I looked up to see them cuddling together on the rug, holding each other ever so sweetly, with Jay speaking softly into her ear.

"What are you guys talking about?"

"Oh, nuffing, Mom!" Austyn grinned.

That's when the two of them came at me from both sides of the island hollering, "Attack!" I couldn't stop laughing as I stole a pillow to fight back.

The two of them are always tickle-fighting, exploring the neighborhood together, and getting into mischief. I love that Jay definitely still has a solid relationship with his "inner child." The older Austyn gets, the more thankful I am for that because it really does help having two of us to keep up with her.

Ever since Jay became a permanent fixture in our lives, he and I have shared Austyn's bedtime duties, normally tackling them together. As my baby belly continued to swell, we relished the time with just the three of us, knowing we would have to do a lot more tag-teaming once the baby came.

"Okay! What do you want to talk about?" I asked, tucking Austyn's blanket she'd had since she was a baby a little tighter around her, just as she liked.

Most nights, Austyn used her allotted "talk time" (a Nick-and-me tradition I vowed to keep alive) to her advantage, making up silly questions about all kinds of things just to keep us in the room longer and ward off sleep. But that night it felt different. She seemed to be thinking very hard about something. She looked at me first, then at my ever-growing tummy housing her very-hard-prayed-for little sister, and finally her eyes settled right on Jay.

"When can I go to my Daddy Nick's house? I haven't been there before, and I really want to go and spend the night." Her sweet face broke into a small hopeful smile.

"Oh, honey . . ." Jay started.

My heart broke a little, knowing there was no way her four-year-old mind would be able to understand.

"You can't," he finally said.

I broke in, "He does have a house, though, remember? A nice place where he lives . . . in heaven."

"Well, when can we go there?" she asked, earnestly, her blond hair falling over her eyes.

"Not probably for a long while," I said, glancing at Jay. Tears filled his eyes. I looked away to keep my own from spilling out.

"You said there are golden streets in heaven, right, Mom? So can't we just drive and drive and drive? Just to visit?"

I hated the answer, but we had to give her the truth, which we were having to do more and more, the older she got. We were committed to answering her questions honestly, no matter how hard her questions became.

"No, honey. We can't drive there. If we could, we would definitely go see him," Jay said, brushing her hair aside as he spoke. And I knew he was telling the absolute truth.

A lump caught in my throat as I squeezed her tight. Ever since she was a baby, all I wanted was to protect her. I was so glad to know our Creator was working toward the same end goal. The loss this little girl had already endured, one she still didn't fully understand, broke my heart.

"What's awesome is, one day . . ." I cleared my throat, trying to keep my voice level. "We will be able to go to Daddy Nick's house, and it will be such a wonderful time. The *best* time you've ever had!"

"Are you sure?" Austyn sighed and frowned.

"Absolutely!" I said with conviction. Because I am so very sure.

"It will be the best. Like a party! Right, Mom?" She started to smile. "I remember now . . . it *will* be the *best!*" Her voice grew stronger with every word. "Because I have three daddies who can be at the party with me!" Austyn smiled even bigger, practically shouting in victory over her predicament. She loved telling anyone who would listen that she had "three daddies!"

"I have God in heaven. I have my Daddy Nick in heaven. And I have my dad—you!" She dramatically pointed at Jay, a huge grin spreading across her face. Then she turned her finger right toward my tummy. "Plus, my little baby sister! Yay! Yay! Yay!"

"Yup! You'll always have your family. Forever and ever." Jay reached over and pulled her right into his lap for a tickle fest.

I laughed so hard at the two of them that tears escaped, but I didn't mind. I couldn't always tell any more if they were happy or sad tears. More often than not, they were a mix of both. The bittersweet days were fine by me; the depth in my life was worth every single drop.

As my thirtieth birthday approached, a sense of gratitude coursed through me.

Every year that passed without Nick, the milestones seemed to involve less grief and more intention given toward living a life worthy of the air I was using up. Still, there are a few times a year Jay almost expects to find me cozied up at home with a box of tissues. He's always supportive, loving, and never pushy, and often brings me flowers or ice cream and gives me plenty of alone time.

At first he wasn't sure how to deal with my waves of grief, but eventually we talked through what might be best for both of us. I warned him in advance that it's not predictable. And it's not normally the milestone date itself, but typically the days leading up to it. He knows Nick and I never broke up and never will. He knows I will never stop loving either of them. For that, I am eternally grateful.

My pity parties used to last for a week or more, but I can tell I'm making progress. At five years out, after lots of personal development and prayer, I've almost been able to decide how long I'll *allow* myself to flounder in the darkness.

I don't think we should ever try to get over something or someone on a certain timeline or try to move on; we should only move *forward*. We can take a part of our experience with us and choose to do the best we can with this new part of us here and the other part of us missing. I'm definitely not saying I deserve some sort of gold medal for the way I've dealt with my grief. Every journey is different, none better than the other. But I do believe it's made a huge difference that I recognize I have a choice. I can choose to wallow in self-pity, or I can choose to reframe the scenario.

I never got the miracle I hoped for with Nick. He didn't get to stay on this earth long enough to see his baby girl grow up. But I believe Nick's going to heaven was a miracle in itself. He is now fully alive and pain free, and we will see him again soon. Knowing Nick is in a better place absolutely helps. But I don't believe my heart will ever fully settle comfortably around the way this world works.

I know one day complete clarity will outshine any doubts I've ever held, and I look forward to that. In the meantime, I'm determined to live my life bravely, with intention, taking action, looking for miracles, dispensing hope as often as I can, choosing kindness, and spreading love. I'd rather do that than wallow in self-pity anyway. I know that's what Nick would have wanted for me; more importantly, I know this is the life I was made for.

Emery Rose was born on March 21, 2018, just five days before her big sister's fifth birthday. Eyes as blue as her dad's, she weighed 7 lbs., 10 oz., and was 21 inches long. She was perfect, she was beautiful, and she was everything the meaning of her name implied—"brave." My heart expanded all over again that day, just like the Grinch's but better, making room enough to fit yet another all-consuming, never-ending love.

Seeing my girls together for the first time was one of the greatest joys I will ever experience in this lifetime. My first daughter was born into a world straining from the weight of impending loss. My second was born into a world bursting with all the hope of a new beginning.

The contrast was rich, and the beauty of the future that was just beginning to come into focus for our little patched-up family was clear. There was no way I could have pictured a life so full of love for myself. None other than the Creator of the universe could have orchestrated it all to come together in a way as full circle as this.

Once we were alone in our hospital room on the night of Emery's birth, when Em had peacefully drifted off to sleep, I'd turned to Jay and just about crumpled into his embrace as overwhelming gratefulness washed over me.

"You did good, beautiful." Jay looked at me in awe, and I couldn't keep the grateful tears from falling once again. I thought about the incredible gift this life is—both the good and the bad parts. Somehow I knew, as incredible as everything already was, the best was still to come. The love of my Creator had changed absolutely everything about me. Life was no longer happening to me. I was not an innocent bystander, watching events unfold. Instead, I could finally trust with all my heart that He would continue to make sure everything in my life (the good and the bad) would happen entirely for me.

Because I knew He loved me that darn much. Because I knew I was made for brave.

"How do you feel right now?" Jay asked.

"One word?" I took a deep breath and said, "Blessed."

Author's Note

I TRIED AND FAILED to write versions of this book for years. Every time I sat down to the keyboard to type, my thoughts turned to molasses. Writing felt like pulling teeth, and I've never been very fond of the dentist.

After a number of botched attempts, years ago I told God I wouldn't be trying to write this story anymore. It was nothing but frustrating. I was done. My timing was obviously off. Maybe there were some lesson I still had yet to learn that belonged in these pages. Maybe there was more to the story I had yet to live. I told God, "If it's supposed to happen, You will have to make it blaringly obvious."

There aren't many times in my life where I would swear I heard God speak audibly. But, when I caught the words "It's time" during worship at a church service in the fall of 2017, I knew exactly who had uttered them.

Never mind that it was the *worst* timing as far as I was concerned. I was busier than I had ever been trying to be an exceptional wife, a present mother, running a business, raising a preschooler, *and* extremely pregnant with my second daughter. But, according to God, it was time to tell my story, so I listened and started taking action.

The words flowed like honey, pouring out of me seemingly of their own accord, cascading over the pages until words turned to sentences and sentences turned to pages. The first draft of the manuscript had enough content for not just one book but two and was done in a matter of three months. In true alignment, everything for this project moved together more beautifully than I could have ever hoped.

Even after all God had done in my life, I almost couldn't believe what happened next.

Back in 2013, when we first published Nick's video on YouTube just before he entered hospice care, his video had reached 1,000 views. Nick had been thrilled and humbled, and his eyes had welled over with tears when I told him. The encouraging comments from a couple hundred people made him weep.

"I told you this would all be worth it if we impacted *one* life, love . . . *one*." Tears ran down his cheeks. "This is *one thousand!*" he said, smiling wide.

We got a stream of letters and emails and messages of thanks while Nick was sick. People kept telling us how much of a difference his video made in their lives and their faith. Multiple people told us they'd accepted Jesus for the first time or recommitted their lives to God. Nick cried tears of joy every single time we heard from someone new.

But the video hadn't really even scraped its potential until after Nick passed away in January of 2014. I was amazed when I logged on one day to see over 100,000 views! I could imagine Nick in heaven jumping for joy. The comments were endless and hope was spreading.

When someone asked permission to translate Nick's words into Spanish, I gave the green light. When a few others emailed with requests for German, French, and more, I said, "Yes!" over and over again. Then I watched in absolute awe as the video made its way around the world, garnering over a million views. I couldn't imagine anything more humbling.

But it seems the very second God told me it was time to write this book was the same moment He decided to really prove to me all that He was capable of. Long after the original was filmed, and over five years after Nick died, Nick's video took off in a way it never had before . . . over half a decade after it was first published.

One hundred million views . . . (and counting). 100,000,000. That's a whole lot of views, my friend.

If that's not proof our Creator can make good out of bad, then I don't know what is.

We know that all things work together for the good of those who love God, who are called according to his purpose.

—Romans 8:28

Join the Movement

MY DEAR FRIEND,

If you've been waiting for permission to make changes in your life and the rest of this book didn't serve as enough of a sign, I'm giving you permission now!

Life is too short to stay the same. And all you have to do is start with one bold step in the right direction. You don't have to move on from your hurt, your questions or your fear. But, you *have* to move forward. Because you won't experience that peace of knowing who you are and what you were made for, until you take the first step toward it.

For me, that first step was truly accepting the love of my Creator and His goodness. That one decision changed absolutely everything.

I've walked through the valley of the shadow of death and risen out of the depths of grief more grateful and alive than ever before. I recognize now that perhaps the reason I was asked to climb these mountains was so I could show you it could be done.

If you want to dive deeper in your own journey, if you want to see miracles in your own life, if you're ready to take a leap of faith that I promise can begin turning everything around for good, consider starting with this prayer. "Jesus, I give you my life."

If you prayed this prayer, that isn't where the conversation ends. This is where the conversation begins. You and your Creator probably have a lot to talk about. And this beautifully brave heart-to-heart will go on for eternity.

If that step feels too bold or too scary right now, that's okay too. He'll wait for you. But, start asking the hard questions now, start diving deeper to figure out what you believe, and spend time each day in your own "soul study" looking for the answers that matter to you. Maybe even consider starting the Soul Study Guide I created to go along with this book.

Being "made for brave" means knowing you were made for something more and that you were built brave enough to do hard things. Spread the hope and show us you are #MadeforBrave too by sharing the hashtag on social media. Don't forget to tag me @alyssagalios so I can cheer you on and celebrate with you!

No matter what you might choose your next step to be, know this: *You are already loved. You are forever wanted.* The plan is already in place. The door is already there, waiting to be opened. You just have to believe all this good is true and grab the key.

Be present. Be good. And be brave, my friend. You were made for this.

xo,

Alyssa

Giving Back

ONE HUNDRED PERCENT OF the net proceeds from this book are being donated to causes close to our Made for Brave hearts, including those that offer hope to cancer fighters and their families like the Austen Everett Foundation and my friend, Dawn Green's, charity Psuedomyxoma Survivor.

Please visit madeforbrave.com/give for more information on these incredible organizations and their missions.

Acknowledgments

IT TAKES A VILLAGE. I wish I could thank every single person who deserves recognition for the book you have here, but I'm afraid I'd end up with a second book! So from the bottom of my overwhelmingly full heart, I will do my best to list the few people who will fit on these pages. Please offer ample grace if I've accidentally missed some (and know my child is currently experiencing what doctors call "sleep regression"—or what I call "insanity").

You. First, thank you to the thousands and thousands of individuals and communities near and far for your endless love and support. Thank you for reading this book and for every single comment, like, and share that somehow triggered online algorithms to spread a message that I know God intended for the world. *You* were a big part of this.

My family. Specific thanks must go to my sister for answering my endless phone calls about this manuscript and offering wise-beyond-her-years advice. Thank you to my mom for her relentless prayers over my life and this message. Thank you to my brother and sister-in-law for their willingness to help with our girls despite having four of their own. And thank you to my father for asking the hard questions and endlessly encouraging me to believe that someone out there wants to hear what I have to say, even if it's only him.

My friends. A special shout-out to my incredible friends near and far, new and ancient, whose late-night phone calls, wine tastings, pampering parties, text strings and endless adventures kept me sane throughout this process. The good news is you won't have to listen to me talk about writing *this* book much anymore.

My pastor. Endless thanks go to my friend and mentor, Pastor Eric , who still puts up with my calling him "pastor" despite the fact he hasn't been one in the traditional sense for years. Thank you for encouraging me, for loving me, for reading early versions of this book, and endlessly introducing me to unexpected truths and new ways of thinking. Most of all, thank you for gently encouraging me to head right back to where I've always belonged . . . in the arms of Jesus.

My mentors. Thank you to Mike Ma, for making superb connections and always pushing me to make a greater impact while never abandoning his own. Thank you to the wise and wonderful Larry Snyder whose infinite servant heart, cups of coffee, and selfless example I am immensely grateful for.

My team. To those who helped me wrangle my words so the size of this book wouldn't resemble an encyclopedia's, thank you. Thank you to Alisia Leavitt and team, Jennifer Lincoln, and Inger Logelin, specifically on this front. Your red strike-throughs caused panic in my heart, but you should know I love you for them now. Thank you to Athena and the rest of the crew at Redemption Press for believing in this Made for Brave mission and for putting up with my endlessly detailed emails and wordy responses that most likely crossed the line of "too much." This book was my baby, and you made sure she came out right.

My fit family. To our entire larger coaching family and to our Made for Brave community, thank you for helping me confidently spread this message so much further than I might have if left to do it on my own. I am humbled to be a part of what we have created together, and I know this is just the beginning.

My girls. To Austyn Elizabeth, thank you for being fully yourself and sharing your truth without caring who sees. You set a brave example for your momma. To Emery Rose, thank you for your sweet little kicks that kept me awake in the early morning hours as I wrote the first draft for this book—they were far sweeter than a cup of coffee.

My husband. A huge shout-out goes to Jay, the real MVP. Without your constant love and encouragement, I cringe to think of where this book might be. (Probably still in a random file buried in my computer.) Thank you for keeping our kids alive and our business afloat when I've been buried in this manuscript. Thank you for listening to me read and reread the same sentences to you over and over again. Thank you for encouraging me to keep writing even on the worst of days and for showering me with excessive cuddles and endless snacks. You know how desperately I need both to survive. I love you . . . always.

My Creator. Last, but not least, above all others, thank You to God, who had a plan for this story from the very beginning. I've been honored to live it, and I'm humbled to be able to share it here. All for Your glory.

About the Author

ALYSSA GALIOS is an author, motivational speaker, social media influencer and online coach. Founder of the #MadeforBrave movement and CEO of the Made for Brave Company, Alyssa is known for helping countless people create better lives through faith, family, and fitness. Her life story has been featured on countless media outlets like Yahoo News, Christian Post, Fox News, HuffPost, and Viralized. Alyssa and her husband run their business together out of their home office just north of Seattle, Washington where they happily raise their beautifully brave daughters.

Keep up to date with what's going on with #MadeForBrave! Subscribe to AlyssaGalios.com for updates, giveaways, and exciting news.

AlyssaGalios.com